Praise for Previous Books by Walter Doyle Staples:

"Dr. Staples has hit the major issues in personal performance head on. This book, *In Search of Your True Self*, opens your eyes to the critical determinant of happiness and success in life, and shows you how to develop everything you do."

— **Brian Tracy,** author, *Maximum Achievement*

"Leaders are those who have a vision of excellence and have acquired the necessary skills to help themselves and others reach their full potential. By applying the principles in this book, *Think Like a Winner,* you are taking a major step in this direction."

— **Dr. Kenneth Blanchard,**
coauthor, *The One Minute Manager* book series

"*Think Like a Winner* is a scholarly motivational book. It convincingly presents workable formulae for releasing potential."

— **Dr. Norman Vincent Peale,**
author, *The Power of Positive Thinking*

"If you want to maximize your life's potential and at the same time enhance the lives of others, *Think Like a Winner* is vital reading."

— **Dr. Robert H. Schuller,**
former senior pastor, The Crystal Cathedral,
author, *Tough Times Never Last, Tough People Do*

"Dr. Staples has pulled all the magic together from a myriad of sources and blended it in his own special style into a fascinating journey into our minds, hearts, and spirits. We'll all be blessed and inspired by this book (*In Search of Your True Self*)."

— **Les Brown,** author, *Live Your Dreams*

"This book, *In Search of Your True Self,* has an important message: how to master the process of personal empowerment to help ourselves and others live fuller, more productive lives."

— **Denis Waitley,** author, *The Psychology of Winning*

Walter Doyle Staples, PhD

HAPPY 95% OF THE TIME

THREE SIMPLE, PROVEN WAYS TO OVERCOME DEPRESSION AND FEEL CONTENT *ALMOST* ALL OF THE TIME

CAREER PRESS

Pompton Plains, NJ

HAPPY 95% OF THE TIME
EDITED BY JODI BRANDON
TYPESET BY EILEEN MUNSON
Cover design by Brian Moore
Printed in the U.S.A.

To order this title, please call toll-free 1-800-CAREER-1 (NJ and Canada: 201-848-0310) to order using VISA or MasterCard, or for further information on books from Career Press.

The Career Press, Inc.
220 West Parkway, Unit 12
Pompton Plains, NJ 07444
www.careerpress.com

Library of Congress Cataloging-in-Publication Data

CIP Data Available Upon Request.

To my best friend and teacher,
Linda Hull.

Diversity Declaration

A serious effort has been made to provide information in this book that is acceptable to the widest and most diverse group of readers as possible, regardless of race, color, creed, culture, ethnicity, or gender, as well as any particular religious or spiritual following. Any errors or omissions in this regard, whether large or small, are unintentional and remain the sole responsibility of the author. Your suggestions about how to better accommodate these and other aspects of our modern, diverse society in the text are welcome.

Disclaimer

The author of this book does not provide professional medical advice, nor prescribe the use of any particular form of treatment, either directly or indirectly, for any specific medical condition. The primary intent of the author and publisher of this book is to offer insight and information of a general nature to people seeking personal growth and spiritual development. More specifically, it is intended to educate the general population regarding drug-free and clinically proven ways to treat stress, anxiety, and depression—indeed, general and systemic unhappiness—and other related challenges. It is not intended to replace diagnosis and treatment by a recognized healthcare professional of any serious mental condition. If you as a reader of this book choose to use any of the information contained herein, which is your right, neither the author nor the publisher assumes any responsibility for your actions. If you have any concerns whatsoever about the state of your physical, mental, emotional, or spiritual health, you are advised to immediately seek the services of a qualified medical practitioner.

CONTENTS

Part 5:
Knowing About Practical Spirituality
161

Exercise:
The Mind T.R.A.P
221

What does the music in stillness sound like?
I think it is part poetry, part lullaby, and part anthem.
It soars and it soothes; it heralds and it heals.
It is indicative of our Source.

Question and Answer

Question: "Walter, how are you doing?"

Answer: "I'm 95% happy, thank you."

Question: "Wow! That's amazing...
            but why isn't it 100%?"

Answer: "Because, on occasion, I forget who I am.
            Besides, if I was 100% happy all of the time,
            I'd be locked up in a padded room
            with a straitjacket on!"

Authentic Happiness

The happiness that most people know is not the kind that is discussed in this book. We have all experienced happiness from a fortuitous occurrence, a joyous occasion, a successful effort, or a romantic relationship. But happiness from instances such as these is both fleeting and fabricated. It lasts only as long as the event or situation associated with it.

In other words, such happiness comes and goes, and we eagerly look forward to its return. Between these periodic occurrences, however, we often suffer—that is, we are disheartened, disillusioned, or discontent—because we know we are not in total control of our overall mood and state of affairs. We are at the mercy of chance and circumstance, and feel very much at risk.

Following is the definition of happiness—known as *authentic* happiness—that this book is talking about, the kind that is not associated with any aspect of the physical world in which we live. It is a radically different and generally misunderstood kind because of its unique nature: It is predictable, permanent, resplendent, and indestructible. Such happiness is what we all want yet seldom know how to have. But if we can discover a way, we can be happy 95 percent of the time without effort and without fear. Our life is then transformed forever.

Definition

Authentic happiness cannot be purposely created
nor is it a by-product of something else.
It is its own entity. It is spontaneous,
natural, enduring, and enriching.
It comes to the mind, it is not a product of the mind.
It is a clear reflection of our Source.

The Journey Home

Enter Presence; be one with stillness; know you are that.

What is the one, most important question you have, knowing its answer would change your life in many wondrous and unpredictable ways? If one hundred people were asked this, it's likely there would be one hundred different responses. That's understandable; it's not a question most people expect to be asked. First, let me give you my one, most important question, to be followed in this book by my heartfelt, earnest attempt to answer it:

Who am I?

At your core, you know you are not your perceptions, ideas, fantasies, emotions, beliefs, or experiences, because all these mental activities are constantly changing. Grateful one moment, ungrateful the next! Tolerant one moment, intolerant the next! Loving one moment, angry the next! Clearly you are not what is going on in your mind. So perhaps the following, more probing questions are in order:

> Who is my impersonal, unblemished self?
>
> Who is my non-thinking, non-physical self?
>
> Who is my natural, authentic self?

Is there one, definitive answer to all of these questions that doesn't change over time? And if so, is it possible to find it?

You, like most people, are overly concerned with *living* life, failing to realize that you are life. You are the one who is doing all the needless thinking, worrying, and suffering—all the watching and witnessing as you frantically engage with every aspect of the physical world. But who is watching the watcher? Is it possible to stand back, be totally detached, and see yourself do all the watching? If so, who or what is doing that? A final question: Could this also be who you are, your most basic, essential Self?

Once you realize you are not your perceptions, thoughts, mood, or feelings, you have to consider what precedes these often-confusing and hurtful activities. This will also tell you a good deal about the process you will have to follow—and what door to open—if you want to find a substantive answer to the one, key question I have just cited.

Thankfully, as a human being, you are unique and adaptive—indeed evolutionary. You can suspect, introspect, and ponder; you can choose to think or not think (i.e., meditate); and you can conceptualize, contemplate, and evaluate, all in search of truth. From a spiritual perspective, this means you can come to know the Divine and your relationship to it. The answer to my question is now within your grasp. The journey home awaits you.

It is always your mind—and only your mind—
that gets you into trouble; it follows that only your mind
can get you out of it.

The ego in you is destroying your life.
It does this through your mind's compulsive addiction to form.
Simply put, your thoughts are driving you crazy.

Most people believe that the next moment
is more important—and will be more interesting—
than the present moment, the moment at hand.
This, it could be argued,
is the greatest curse of humankind.

Knowing Where to Begin

"If you are easy on yourself, life will be hard on you; if you are hard on yourself, life will be easy on you."

—Zig Ziglar,
motivational speaker;
author of *See You at the Top* (1974)

The Impact of Stress, Anxiety, and Depression

Consider the following comment by Carl Jung (1875–1961), one of the most respected psychiatrists and psychotherapists in the modern era: "It is often tragic to see how blatantly a man bungles his own life and the lives of others yet remains totally incapable of seeing how much the whole tragedy originates in himself, and how he continually feeds it and keeps it going."

I am assuming you agree with this statement yet are also wondering what the solution is, knowing that practically everyone on the planet fits this description. Surely, in this modern age, when you can access all kinds of information with a simple click of a mouse, answers to this problem are self-evident and readily available to all. But, sadly, we know they are not.

At one time or another, you undoubtedly have wondered how you could better manage your thoughts, mood, and feelings—particularly the most hurtful ones—that keep coming your way. Alas, you probably gave up once you discovered the enormity and complexity of the task. And so the pain and suffering you knew in the past continue to be a part of your life today.

Many believe that pain and suffering are unavoidable and inevitable, that they are just part of the human condition. The headlines in the daily news seem to support this view. *Yet I submit to you they are not.* As proof, I invite you to explore with me several exciting options that are available to anyone who wants to escape from the trap that Jung notes we have set for ourselves. It seems only logical that if we are smart enough to set the trap and keep it going, we are also smart enough to dismantle it and shut it down.

Is it really possible to be happy 95 percent of the time? And if so, how, what is the process? The process involves critically analyzing, understanding, and learning from our past experiences, and finding specific and proven ways to overcome their potentially harmful and often-debilitating effects. What follows is a description of my efforts to deal with adversity and depression in my own life, including new research findings that confirm the efficacy of the top-three known cures for depression (listed on pages 36–37). While testing each of these approaches thoroughly over many months and years, I have found that they bear the desired fruit if properly cultivated and carefully nourished.

So here is my invitation: These are the steps I took. They worked for me. But will they work for you? You will have to try them yourself to find out. We know all Beings carry within them the seeds of their own enlightenment.

Was the process easy? No. Did all the pieces fall nicely together in a timely and orderly manner? No. Was there a lot of help available to me in my community? No. Was my immediate family able to help? No. Most lived far away, were all busy, and didn't have any deep insight into the matter anyway. Not surprisingly, they were as ill-informed on the subject as I was.

Because I had just moved to where I was living at the time, I didn't have a family doctor but was able to get a local hospital to put me on a nine-month waiting list to see a psychiatrist. (Geez, that was easy. It only required sitting and crying for six or seven hours in ER on three different occasions at three different hospitals!) Hence my only recourse was to proceed on my own to deal with the matter. And so I did. Necessarily, this made the whole process longer and more difficult, but it also had its own rewards.

The approaches described here to treat depression can bring relief in a relatively short period of time (i.e., a few weeks or months) but this requires your own active participation as well as some outside professional help. For your part, you will be asked to think and rethink in order to undo several of your habitual ways of thinking, adopt new lifestyle choices, and be much easier and kinder toward your "self." Like most people, you are undoubtedly your own worst critic, and think you are undeserving and incapable of making major changes in your life. But as will be shown, you are wrong.

The material here does not include a discussion about the use of prescription drugs to treat various mood disorders and depression, although they can be useful in some cases. Such drugs have serious drawbacks. It often takes several attempts to find the right one. Drugs work for only about 50 percent of patients, and those who do experience improvement often have to stay on them indefinitely to avoid a relapse. Finally, drugs are not a viable option for many people because of serious side effects that can include lethargy, cognitive impairment, and sexual dysfunction.

My Source of Motivation

My motivation for writing this book lies in having witnessed as well as having experienced depression in my own life, and wanting to find more effective and better ways to understand it and move beyond it. As a child in the 1950s, I witnessed my mother's pain during periodic bouts of depression. As a husband, I have witnessed my wife's ongoing struggle with bipolar disorder, first diagnosed in 1981. As a father, I have witnessed my daughter's difficulties dealing with anxiety, claustrophobia, and panic attacks.

Later, specifically in 1999, it was my turn. I spent a full year in a deep clinical depression characterized by spontaneous fits of crying for several hours a day. Suicidal thoughts were my constant companion. At the time, I had no idea what had brought on the depression (although I had some strong hints), or any idea how to deal with it or get out of it. I was literally lost, out of control, trying to stay afloat in a vast sea of darkness, desolation, and deep despair. I didn't know at the time that about one in five people experiences a major depression at some point in his life.

Once I had recovered and saw how difficult this process actually was, I knew I never wanted to go through such an experience again. As a result, I began an extensive and fruitful study that took me down many roads and in several directions. I ended up researching and writing about 1,000 hours a year for 15 years, or 15,000 hours. The result is this book and an earlier, related one, titled *May the Healing Begin,* which was published in 2010. For me, it has been an exciting and rewarding journey. I am grateful for having this opportunity to share my findings with you.

Wayne W. Dyer came out with a book and CD program in 2001 called *There's a Spiritual Solution to Every Problem.* What an interesting title,

I thought, as well as a powerful inspirational concept. It immediately attracted my attention. It helped me better understand what I needed to do and what path I needed to follow. Indeed, as my research progressed, I found that Dr. Dyer was right: There is a spiritual solution to every problem. That was one of several "a-ha!" moments for me.

In addition to Dr. Dyer, I am indebted to Aaron T. Beck, MD; Herbert Benson, MD; David D. Burns, MD; Deepak Chopra, MD; David Doidge, MD; Dr. Albert Ellis; Carl Jung, MD; Dr. Jon Kabat-Zinn; Maxwell Maltz, MD; Dr. Jordan Peterson; Dr. Zindel Segal; Eckhart Tolle; Neale Donald Walsch; and Marianne Williamson for helping me on my own journey. The following comment by Canadian writer and philosopher Ronald Cole (1942–2009) was also helpful: "Few are those who walk on water; most of us are simply fortunate enough to find stones that someone else has placed in life's pond and tread on them when the need arises."

Yes, the world is hurting, our communities are hurting, our places of work are hurting, our friends and loved ones are hurting, and you and I are hurting, all to different degrees but certainly for similar reasons. And we know for a fact that this hurt (i.e., emotional pain and suffering) is deepening and growing, not diminishing. This is why I took the steps I did to learn what is described in this book. If you have similar challenges or want to help others with theirs, I suggest you need to do the same thing.

Facts and Findings

Here are some important facts and findings to consider:

* Mental disorders of various kinds have become a world-wide phenomenon, a pandemic with no borders. The World Health Organization (WHO) currently states on its Website that anxiety is "the most prevalent mental health problem across the globe."

* Researchers today better understand the full impact of stress on the body. They know it can lead to depression, Alzheimer's disease, obesity, diabetes, heart disease, and sexual dysfunction.

✳ Everyday events that are novel, unpredictable, or threatening—either to the ego or your very survival—trigger a stress response. This is the primitive fight-or-flight response that in turn releases two powerful hormones, namely cortisol and adrenalin.

✳ These hormones change the way the body stores fat, leading to higher rates of obesity and an increase in the production of cholesterol and insulin, which leads to heart disease and diabetes.

✳ A recent study in Canada found that, on average, a person has 14 stressful episodes per week. Clearly your first order of business is to reduce your level of stress in both your personal and professional life.

✳ The same study found that hypertension (high blood pressure) is the number-one reason why people go to see their doctor in the first place; in 2009, it accounted for 20.7 million medical appointments. Extrapolating based on population, the figure is probably close to 200 million in the United States.

✳ Stress affects our places of work as well; there has been a 21-percent increase in absentee rates in the past decade. In 2009, stress-related absences from work cost employers in Canada more than $10 billion a year, with an additional $14 billion impact on the healthcare system. The U.S. figure is likely close to $250 billion.

✳ Chronic stress reduces the size of your brain, namely the hippocampus. It's the region responsible for memory formation and is linked directly to Alzheimer's disease. In general, chronic stress negatively affects your immune system, thus allowing diseases to take hold that normally would be fended off.

(Source: Agrell, Siri. "Stress: How Your Busy Life is Killing You" (*The Globe and Mail,* October 30, 2010.)

Other findings regarding teens and young adults:

❋ Out of 25 students in a classroom, one in five has seriously considered attempting suicide, more than one in six has made plans to attempt suicide, and more than one in 12 has made a suicide attempt in the past year.

❋ Female teens are more likely to attempt suicide than males, but male teens are four times more likely to succeed.

❋ More than 90% of teen suicide victims have a mental disorder such as depression or a history of substance abuse. Many mental illnesses, including depression, that contribute to suicide risk appear to have a genetic component.

❋ In a study at Michigan State University reported in February 2011, the primary reason why students quit college was depression. The study involved a survey of 1,158 freshmen at 10 U.S. colleges and universities.

❋ About 100 million Americans are taking prescription drugs of one kind or another. This is close to one-third of the total population.

❋ There were 38,364 suicides in the United States in 2010, an average of 105 each day. Up to 20 percent of these were veterans of foreign wars. This resulted in $34.6 billion in combined medical and other related costs.

❋ Worldwide, experts estimate there are about 2,500 suicides per day, or about 912,500 every year. In other words, every four or five years, there goes Philadelphia, there goes Chicago, or there goes Toronto. (Note: Countries vary widely in their ability and willingness to track and report suicides.)

(Sources: (1) *www.safeyouth.org/scripts/teens/suicide.sap.*
(2) National Youth Violence Prevention Resource Center (NYVPRC); (3) Centers for Disease Control and Prevention's (CDC) Morbidity and Mortality Weekly Report; (4) *sciencedaily. com/releases/2011/02.*)

Authentic Happiness

Most people lack a detailed understanding of what "everyday" happiness actually is, its many sources, whether they are external or internal, and the amount in each case. True, we know it can come from at least eight different sources. They include: (1) loved ones in the immediate family (the couple, their children, their parents, and their siblings); (2) extended family; (3) friends and acquaintances; (4) career; (5) finances; (6) physical well-being; (7) mental well-being; and (8) spiritual well-being. All of these sources of happiness vary in depth, intensity, frequency, and duration (i.e., temporary versus permanent), and seldom is a person 100 percent happy 100 percent of the time. (Oops! This is one definition of insanity.)

Everyday happiness can also be categorized another way. There are *extrinsic* or materialistic, ego-based sources that include money, possessions, titles, positions, awards, etc.; and there are *intrinsic* or spiritual-based sources that are directly associated with unconditional, transcendent love. Intrinsic sources in turn help develop positive and enriching character traits that include acceptance, compassion, understanding, gratitude, kindness, joyfulness, humility, patience, tolerance, and deep peace. These traits, and others like them, represent authentic happiness because they reflect the essence and permanence of our actual Being.

As well, there is often only one source of happiness that is dominant at any one point in time. For example, this could be physical prowess/well-being for a young, attractive movie star or an accomplished athlete; mental prowess/well-being for a mathematician or an accomplished writer/artist; or spiritual prowess/well-being for an enlightened, perceptive person who has taken time to grow spiritually. As one source begins to fade, such as physical attractiveness or mental prowess, we promptly look for another one to take its place. Necessarily, this can be a difficult transition for many people.

It's useful to look back and see what your sources of everyday happiness (which in turn directly affects your sense of "self") actually were at various stages in your life, whether they were extrinsic or intrinsic, and the level in each case. I share with you my own assessment here: (In each case, the number has been rounded off to the nearest 5 percent.)

	In My Mid-20s	In My Mid-40s	In My Mid-60s
Immediate Family:	25%	35%	10%
Extended Family:	5%	0%	0%
Friends:	15%	10%	5%
Career:	30%	40%	0%
Finances	5%	5%	5%
Physical:	15%	5%	5%
Mental:	5%	5%	5%
Spiritual:	0%	0%	75%

From this it's clear that the major changes for me include "Immediate Family" going from an average of 30 to 10 percent; "Friends" decreasing substantially; "Career" going to absolute zero; and "Spiritual" going from zero for most of my life to fully 75 percent today. (P.S. At the time of my death, I predict "Spiritual" will be 100 percent, reflecting a deep and abiding love for all things.) I suggest you conduct this same exercise yourself, and see what levels and trends apply to you. Of particular interest would be whether there has been a significant decrease in extrinsic sources of everyday happiness and an offsetting increase in intrinsic sources.

It's So Easy to Do Nothing

I often wonder why people like to hang out in their comfort zone all the time—why they cling so strongly to repetition, regularity, and predictability, all aimed at avoiding change. Perhaps it's because human nature always takes the path of least resistance. Most people are quite content with their present situation. They know where they live, where they work, they know their friends, their families, they know their strong points, their weak points, they know what makes them happy, what makes them sad; they have become addicted to the status quo, to the way things are. And so they just hunker down, avoid risk, and hope for the best. Then, when bad (meaning unwelcome) things happen, they are easy victims and find themselves lost in a morass of negativity, despair, and often total helplessness.

Why else might people be so afraid of change, including bringing about change in themselves? In part, it may simply be fear of the unknown. This is understandable, but you need to realize change will happen anyway—that it's beyond your control. Change is simply what life is all about. Knowing this leads to another realization, namely that change in your life can occur in only one of two ways: First, it can and will happen *to you,* and you have no choice in the matter; and second, it can happen *by you,* and here you have total control over the way you go about it, what tools to use, and at what pace you wish to proceed.

The wise among us already know this. Such people bring about as much change as they can both in themselves and in their circumstances, knowing that change both good and bad will invariably show up all by itself and impose itself on them. Note that the world will not slow down, nor will change stop, just because you want to get off the train. Change is both constant and inevitable. It will go on and on, and often at a faster and faster pace. If you get in the way and don't know how to deal with it, it will simply run you over. The result? You will end up as expendable roadkill, just another number in a non-descript statistics table.

Most people are hesitant about taking on a new, seemingly major challenge of any kind—including personal growth and spiritual development—one that is in addition to all the other challenges they already have. After all, it's both a lot of hard work—that can't be much fun—and they just might fail, and failure isn't something most people look forward to. They know failure happens frequently enough. Do they really want another one to beat them up even more?

Yet failure is a wonderful teacher, perhaps even the very best one. That's because it is through failure that you get one step closer to getting things right. This applies both to improved cognitive thinking skills as well as a deeper understanding of who and what you are—your true Nature. If you learn about and earnestly apply just one important new approach or principle, you are ahead of the game because now you can manage your circumstances and your life just a little bit better. As a result, you will end up making better decisions and these decisions, both big and small, determine how well your life unfolds. This, then, needs to be your perspective and it is how I suggest you should proceed.

New Conceptions of Reality

Consider for a moment this comment by Dr. Jordan Peterson, professor of psychology at the University of Toronto. In one of his lectures, he points out the many serious problems that the world is facing today—meaning the serious problems many people are facing today—and he says, "It's important to make your *conceptions of reality* more sophisticated. You want to do that because you have to live in the world. And the more sophisticated your conceptions are, the less likely you'll encounter tragic or harmful circumstances that you'll be unable to deal with. And so it really matters *what you're thinking* and you know *how to think.*" (author's emphasis)

Here, Professor Peterson makes two important points. First, he says you should be aware of the thoughts you are having at any point in time (i.e., what you're thinking), and second, he says you need to know the (two) very different ways how to think, namely the "active" and the "passive" modes of mind. The vast majority of people don't meet either of these criteria, and as a result live lives filled with ongoing pain and suffering, often resulting in recurring bouts of depression and deep despair.

So what is the solution here? Everything you understand about your world—everything!—is a direct result of the workings of your mind. And we know your mind can do only two things: *think* and *not think.* Clearly it's critical that you learn how to improve on—indeed master—these two important skills, for if you master your mind, you master your world. This, then, will be our focus—understanding and applying the two different ways to think that are available to you to make your life more magical, more memorable, and more meaningful.

You Have to Pay a Price

There is a certain price you have to pay to become more informed and enlightened, namely some serious study over many months or even years. And yes, there are significant rewards, including an end to pain and suffering, although this is only one of the many rewards you will reap.

Ask yourself this: How much does the average book weigh? About 1 pound? Surely this is not too heavy a load to bear. Is a pound, the weight of the average book, very heavy compared to the weight of all the pain and suffering you are currently carrying around? Do you have an 800-pound gorilla strapped firmly to your back, representing all the simmering and debilitating hurts, fears, anger, guilt, and regret you have acquired over the years? Do you realize a single, 1-pound book can take them off?

My fervent hope is that this discussion will turn into a commitment by you to do some heavy lifting, so to speak—some serious work on your *self*. You see, when your little self (lowercase s), which is the ego, gets out of the way and allows your true Self (capital S), meaning your Source, to intercede and guide you, miracles both large and small begin to happen. And a life sprinkled with miracles here and there is surely one that is worth living.

Perhaps the greatest miracle you will ever experience in your life is this: a switch from ignorance to understanding, from doubt to certainty, and from fear to love. Indeed, if this happens—responding to situations with love when before you reacted to them with fear and trepidation, or even anger—things will be a lot better in your life regardless of what challenges you may face in the future.

We know what the future holds. This includes wars being waged, revolts being planned, riots being instigated, murders being committed, robberies being carried out, rapes being perpetrated, power being abused, frauds being conceived, lies being told, divorces being filed, alcohol being consumed, drugs being taken, and bribes being paid, all causing pain and suffering to be inflicted. All do their part to negatively impact the lives of average people regardless of race, color, creed, gender, age, education, income, or religious affiliation. Yes, pain and suffering, both individual and collective, are very much part of our modern world. But as will be shown, they are all—at their core—a direct result of illogical, irrational, or erroneous (i.e., faulty, selfish, and often callous) thinking.

Think about it. How many of the problems in the world today—indeed during the long course of human history—are a result of a few people wanting to feel important and willing to go to any extreme to achieve it? Is such an approach either logical and rational, or fair and reasonable? No. Rather it is a person's over-sized ego on the rampage, out of control, oblivious, and unconcerned about the consequences of its actions. The ego is the consummate stealth weapon. Silently, secretly, without being noticed, it can—and often does—cause immense damage, severe pain, and deep suffering, both self-inflicted and otherwise.

Make Self-Healing Your Priority

Many believe that a majority of people in the world today are quite mad, meaning they are not aware of the two kinds of thinking that are available to them. This causes them to suffer from a "not-able-to-stop-thinking" impediment, a debilitating affliction, yet few of us realize this because we all have it! It's really an all-consuming, self-inflicted, and self-limiting *disease*. Constant, compulsive thinking is what keeps us locked into the physical world, into the world of thought and form, one that's of little substance and very often pure nonsense. In other words, if our actual being is hidden from us, we are living blind to the truth, blind and ignorant regarding who we are.

This book is a serious effort to deal with this important challenge. It represents a unique opportunity to begin healing yourself, as well as doing your part to help heal the world in which you live. I like the saying "If it is to be, it's up to me." Why? Because it puts the responsibility for your well-being and situation in life squarely on your shoulders, right where it should be. It's your life, and it rests with you to make it as meaningful, joyful, and productive as possible.

So when should you get started? Well, you could wait and simply hope things will get better in your life all by themselves, with no effort on your part. Good luck with that! Instead, I suggest you take the initiative and start today. Why procrastinate and suffer yet another day, another week, another month, or another year? Let me applaud and commend you as you begin this journey. It may well be like no other you will ever have.

"I have been there—the lowest of the lows, and have suffered from that, the excruciating and debilitating pain. Now, after working very, very hard, I know I will never be in that position again."

—The Author

"A psychological transformation is not possible without a spiritual awakening, and before a man can change his kind of thinking, it first is necessary that he alters his conception of self."

—U.S. Andersen (1917–1986),
American author of *Three Magic Words* (1954)

"I do not feel obliged to believe that the same God who has endowed us with sense, reason and intellect has intended us to forgo their use."

—Galileo Galilei (1564–1642),
Italian physicist, mathematician, astronomer, and philosopher

"Some men covet knowledge out of a natural curiosity and inquisitive temper;

some to entertain the mind with variety and delight;

some for ornament and reputation;

some for victory and contention; many for lucre and a livelihood;

and but few for employing the divine gift of reason to the use and benefit of mankind."

—Sir Francis Bacon (1561–1626),
English philosopher, scientist, essayist, and statesman;
author of *New Atlantis* (1624)

My Commitment

You cannot see the light until you begin to walk the path.

My commitment is to help you get to a new place—a place of lasting peace, inner joy, and serenity. This involves three steps. First, I will introduce you to the top three cures for depression known today that in turn lead to greater awareness, understanding, and self-realization. Both individually and collectively, these approaches help sufferers move from resignation to revelation, from superficiality to substance. In the order they are discussed in the text, they include:

* **Cognitive-behavioral therapy (CBT),** often called "talk" therapy or psychotherapy, with the critical thinking it involves.

❋ **Mindfulness-meditation therapy (MMT),** and how it connects you to the serenity and solace of your Source.

❋ **Practical-spirituality therapy (PST),** and its related self-image psychology component that in essence says: You become in your life the person you see yourself to be in your mind.

You need to know that you have an element of choice here. You don't have to master all three of these approaches at the same time in order to achieve the results you desire. As has been stated, *each one by itself is a known cure for depression,* whether mild or severe. For example, perhaps practical spirituality doesn't appeal to you at the present time. Fine. We all approach life and its many challenges differently and at our own pace. My advice? Focus on what interests you the most right now and where you think you can achieve the best results. Interest in other areas may follow later.

More importantly, you don't even have to be suffering from depression—or any mental disorder—to benefit significantly from any or all of these practices. People in general, whether their life situation is currently positive or negative, find that they enjoy a higher quality of life if they improve on *the way they think.* This, then, as you entertain each thought and experience each moment, needs to be your main focus and top priority. As will be shown on many occasions, the way you think is the key to a new reality.

An explanation of each of these enabling tools comprises key segments in the text, and together necessarily make up the core of the book. By understanding and applying them, you will come to see how the mind works and in turn how it actually creates your reality, meaning how you see yourself and your world, and how you can prosper, grow, and excel in it.

Second, I will walk you through a series of exercises (Annexes 1 through 15) that are presented at various points. This gives you the opportunity to directly apply theoretical concepts to certain challenges you may now have. In the process, you will understand the concepts better and learn how to use them more effectively on a daily basis in order to move ahead.

Third, toward the end of the book, I will introduce the Mind T.R.A.P. and, through critical analysis, show you how your current way of thinking can be negatively impacting your mind and seriously limiting your progress. You are encouraged to repeat the same exercise described there for each and every hurtful issue you may currently be experiencing, whether there are three, four, or five of them. Naturally this will take some time and effort, and that's fine. The result will be the same: knowing at your core that you are love—pure, resplendent, transcendent love.

This is the transformational process we will be exploring together, and it lies in utilizing the unlimited faculties of your mind to best advantage. More specifically, this requires knowing, first, how to *think* and second, and even more importantly, how to *not think*. The former involves practicing the key skill called critical thinking, and the latter involves tapping into the richness and vastness of universal mind through regular, daily meditation.

It has been known for centuries that if you tap into the stillness within, to the place of no thoughts, your mind moves beyond the "active" mode of thinking to the "passive" mode of not thinking. In the process, by spending time in stillness—in the moment, in Now—you will find many positive changes will come into your life that can be had no other way. Among these changes, many of which are described on page 146, you will find the lasting peace, inner joy, and serenity that we have been talking about.

As we begin to explore ways to bring about a meaningful—indeed transformational—change in consciousness, the word *theosophy* is of note. As a noun, theosophy is defined as *any of various philosophies or religious systems that propose to establish direct contact with divine principle through contemplation, revelation, etc., and to gain thereby a spiritual insight superior to empirical knowledge.* (Note: All definitions in the text are from *Webster's New World Dictionary.*)

Mere thinking is not the highest state of mind.

The highest state of mind is no-mind.

Ironically, thinking often leads us no-where

and no-mind leads us very much some-where.

Sadly, most of us think too much too much of the time.

How to Live the Authentic Life

You need to better understand the process you use to think. The reason is simple:

> *The very first step in everything you do—or don't do—in life begins with the thoughts you choose and give the most importance to.*

Of course, you can have exciting thoughts and feel excited, then act on them; or you can have depressing thoughts and feel depressed, and do little or nothing. So which of these two scenarios appeals to you the most? I think I know your answer. You want to manifest a lifetime of accomplishment and fulfillment, to do the things that make a difference in your life and in the lives of others. You now have this incredible opportunity—to live in a state of sustained happiness and well-being on a continuous basis!

Happy 95% of the Time presents a definitive, broad-based approach to managing and controlling your everyday thoughts, mood, and feelings. It's a fascinating look at how you can live more fully and positively, and learn more about yourself and your world, and your rightful place in it. I draw on several important disciplines—behavioral psychology, philosophy, theology, sociology, anthropology, science, and others (i.e., common sense)—to make my main point, namely that you are a spiritual being living in a physical world, yet many either don't know this or don't fully accept it.

As a consequence, many people are not genuinely happy. They lack meaning, purpose, and direction, and a sense of passion in their lives. They feel unfulfilled, unworthy, and unappreciated. They are not content; they are not at ease; they are not themselves. They often suffer from a host of debilitating ailments that can include fear, hurt, anger, guilt, regret, desperation, and despair, along with the many serious physical illnesses that these mental afflictions can bring on, including high blood pressure, heart disease, diabetes, and cancer.

This necessarily limits their ability to live and function as they should, including their relationships with family and friends, their jobs and career, their finances, their personal goals and aspirations—indeed, their ability to live abundantly and productively as vibrant, creative, and joyous human beings. From all this, it's clear that when both your mental and physical health are at risk, nothing else in your life can work very well.

To support this main point—that you can be happy 95 percent of the time—I use timeless insights, psychological principles, historical anecdotes, personal experiences, clinical research findings, humorous quips, and insightful quotations from dozens and dozens of learned people in all walks of life—most very common folk who possess very uncommon knowledge.

I explain that the underlying intent of all the great spiritual masters—from Lao-tzu and Buddha to Jesus and Mohammed—is remarkably similar: to encourage people to direct their hearts and minds *inward* toward the Divine (aka God, Presence, or Source), rather than primarily *outward* toward the world of form ("stuff" by whatever name).

I introduce in this book my central concept of hope and happiness in life that has nothing to do with the material world of fame and fortune. Authentic (or genuine) happiness follows naturally and spontaneously from simply understanding who and what you are, your one and only Self, and then deeply and passionately loving that Self. This should be your primary goal.

In turn, this results in something quite remarkable. By acting in harmony with your essence, your innate Nature, you quickly develop an awareness, an understanding, a conscious feeling (some would say an inner *knowing*) of incredible confidence, courage and compassion, coupled with a burning desire to make a difference. Authentic happiness, in fact, is your natural state, but you're not aware of it because you are totally confused, brain-washed, and ill-informed.

Please read on. This book takes you on a single journey but it opens your life to a thousand joys! Indeed, it may be one of the most important books you have ever read.

"This book is guaranteed to inform, inspire, delight, and create wonder in your world. It is an uncommon book for uncommon times. So many people are hurting today, and need the help and encouragement this book so eloquently and beautifully provides."

—The Author

Everyone Is Part of Your Fan Club

Everyone in your life wants you to have peace, hope, happiness, and love as part of your everyday experience. Why? It's because these people fervently believe in you and passionately care about you. As well, everyone benefits—emotionally and otherwise—when you grow, excel, prosper, and succeed. This includes the government, the education system, the health-care industry, your employer, your church, synagogue, or mosque, members of your family, and your close friends. It shouldn't be any surprise that they are all part of your fan club, cheering you on, giving you advice, and wishing you well. However, consider these questions: "Are you aware of this?" "Do you hear what they are saying?" And finally, "Are you accepting personal responsibility to achieve the goals and level of success that you are capable of achieving?" If not, then this may be the book for you!

If you think about it, there are basically two choices available to you as you grow up and mature, and each depends on the particular qualities and values—what are often called character traits—you foster and attract into your life. One leads to a life full of mediocrity and sadness, at best; the other leads to a life full of happiness and fulfillment, at least—even miracles that you cannot begin to imagine. Consider the following:

Your mediocrity shines through when you allow yourself to be consumed by hate, hurt, anger, greed, sadness, guilt, regret, resentment, fear, envy, jealousy, spite, selfishness, cruelty, dishonesty, meanness, superiority, inferiority, pettiness, self-pity, vanity, and false pride. If you adopt these particular traits, there is only one certainty: *You cannot succeed.*

On the other hand, your impeccability shines through when you are infused with hope, happiness, humility, joy, optimism, self-confidence, gratitude, forgiveness, openness, acceptance, serenity, peace, patience, tolerance, compassion, courage, honesty, kindness, generosity, contentment, and a deep sense of wonderment and awe. If you adopt these particular traits, there is only one certainty: *You cannot fail.*

As you go through the book, you will find that the major determining factor regarding which traits you adopt and which ones you do not is how you see yourself, your world, and your proper place in it—in other words, the specific *pictures* or images you have put in your head that you believe represent the real you. This exciting field of study is called self-image psychology. So I encourage you to read on and witness for yourself the process of growing and developing, of understanding and accepting, of achievement and contentment, of hope and happiness, of joy and bliss.

Are There Really Secrets of Success?
I trust the Universe will provide me with all that I need.

Throughout history, humankind has been fascinated by secrets of all kinds and descriptions. Regarding human existence, they have often focused on aspects of either the *physical* domain (i.e., the law of gravity, the speed of light, the atomic structure of matter); the *mental* domain (i.e., the intellect, the conscious state, the unconscious state); or the *spiritual* domain (i.e., the meaning/purpose of life, transcendence, our true Nature). The subject usually has been framed around so-called "secrets of success" and may involve love, hope, happiness, achievement, or the accumulation of great wealth. At other times, it may involve a deeper understanding of life itself (i.e., Who am I? What am I made of? Why am I here?). Deeper still, the question may involve *enlightenment* (i.e., What is it? How can I achieve it? How can I live it on a daily basis?), which may represent the ultimate secret or supreme realization we all want to understand and know more about.

To begin, consider what *enlighten,* the process that leads to enlightenment, actually means. As a verb, enlighten is defined as *(1.) to give the light and fact of knowledge to; reveal truths to; endow with discernment; free from ignorance, prejudice, or superstition; (2.) to inform; give clarification to as to meanings, intentions, etc.; (3.) to light up.*

And what is a secret? A *secret* is defined as *(1.) something known only to a certain person or persons and purposely kept from the knowledge of others; (2.) something not revealed, understood, or explained; (3.) the true cause or explanation, regarded as not obvious: as, secrets of success; (4.) something beyond general knowledge or understanding.*

A film and book titled *The Secret* were released in 2006 by Australian TV writer and producer Rhonda Byrne. Here is Wikipedia's interpretation of the contents: "The tenet of the film and book is that the Universe is governed by a natural law called the law of attraction which is said to work by attracting into a person's life the experiences, situations, events, and people that 'match the frequency' of the person's thoughts and feelings. Therefore, positive thinking and feeling positive are claimed to create life-changing results such as increased health, wealth, and happiness."

Others have offered their insights on secrets as well. Earl Nightingale (1921–1989), American motivational speaker and author, recorded a best-selling audio program in 1956 called *The Strangest Secret* in which he said, "You become what you think about." In A Course in Miracles (1975), it says, "You have no problems, you only think you do." Napoleon Hill (1883–1970) intoned in his book *Think and Grow Rich* (1937), "Whatever the mind of man can conceive and believe, he can achieve." And the Buddha gave us his definition of enlightenment: "It is the end of suffering."

Here are some other pronouncements you may have come across:

* You always create your own reality, which is determined by the quality of your consciousness.

* You already have everything you need to make a miracle of your life. This includes both the tools and the opportunities.

* All secrets, all understandings—all *knowings*—are revealed to you if you go into stillness and simply listen (i.e., ignore the mutterings and machinations of your often malicious mind).

There are many keen observations and deep truths in all of these statements, and together they go some way to help you better understand yourself and the world around you. Based on my own experience and extensive study, however, I believe there are no secrets at all. (I do admit, however, that there are many, many mysteries!) This is because you need only conduct a diligent and systematic search to find meaningful and substantive answers to life's most perplexing questions. Unfortunately few—indeed very few—seem willing to take on this important and life-changing challenge.

As I look around and witness all the pain and suffering that is taking place in our world today, I see a lot of illusion, delusion, and mass confusion, and they all get in the way of your discovering what is true and what is real. These diversions necessarily originate in your mind and have a great deal, if not everything, to do with the ego, and the insidious and destructive role it plays in hiding your true Nature from yourself. I have explained this view in the pages that follow so that you can come up with your own informed opinion on the matter.

Look around you.

How much confusion do you see in nature?

Do not seeds sprout? Do not flowers blossom? Do not rivers flow?

Do not birds sing? Does not the wind blow? Does not the rain fall?

This can only be described as pure perfection, and it abounds everywhere on earth.

This begs the question:

What can you learn from nature to make your own life more perfect, more meaningful, more profound?

You Are Your Own Worst Enemy

Some time ago, Nisargadatta Maharaj (1897–1981), the respected Indian teacher of Advaita Vedanta, shared with us the following affirmation: *"In my world, nothing ever goes wrong."*

This statement stops most people dead in their tracks when they first come across it. NOTHING!!??#*&*#??!! Is that really possible? Just think—what kind of life would you be living if you thought this way? As you go through the text, I suggest you come back periodically and reconsider this statement, and you will see that in fact it is possible. You *can* live in a calm, understanding, forgiving, non-conforming, and non-judgmental way, knowing that everything happens for a reason and a purpose, and in each and every case, it serves you.

Armed with this new awareness, this new understanding, you have to ask yourself, "What could possibly hold me back from being the person I really want to be, from living the life I really want to live, and from achieving the things I really want to achieve?" As you will discover over and over again in this book, the correct answer is—only you! The old adage, "You are your own worst enemy" is 100-percent true. So one of the biggest challenges you face in life can be stated quite simply: "How can you stop being your own worst enemy?" You will find the answer to this question expressed in many different ways and on many different occasions as you read on.

By applying the principles described here, your life will be very different indeed. Consider, for example, the fact that the ego *never* has your best interests in mind. Its primary concerns center around self-aggrandizement and its own survival! So as you go about your day, you need to listen to the ego and what it is telling you. Is its message relevant? Is its message logical, and rational, fair, and reasonable? If not, you need to shut it down—and quickly! You need to ignore its often twisted and self-serving pronouncements, protestations, and rationalizations. (However, a caution: Be aware that the ego is very much like a spoiled, cantankerous child who is used to getting his own way. It isn't about to take *no* for an answer without a ferocious and protracted fight!) This one principle, if practiced consistently and diligently, represents one of the simplest yet most effective approaches to personal well-being and life-long happiness.

Like you, I have had my share of pain and suffering. And like you, I have diligently searched for ways to move beyond such suffering and into deep peace. As all the ancient spiritual masters have discovered and shared with us, there is a way and it is this:

When you let go of the ego, you will be free of your pain.

Once you have a deeper understanding of what this statement actually means and begin to apply it no matter how haltingly in your life, something quite remarkable happens: You will begin to *think* differently, *feel* differently, and hence *behave* differently, and exactly in this order. To use a baseball analogy, this sounds pretty much like a home run to me!

Continuing with this same analogy, let's see what a spiritual home run actually looks like. You begin at home plate just like everyone else, but you feel hurt in your head and heaviness in your heart. So you decide to head off in search of happiness. You soon arrive at first base and begin to *think* differently, and you welcome and acknowledge this as progress. You continue on and find yourself at second base, and begin to *feel* differently.

Great! More progress. Ever more confident, you move on and find your-self at third base, and begin to *behave* differently. Wow—this is so exciting!

As you look up and scan the horizon from this new vantage point, you see what you know as "home" is not too far off. So you move in that direction and soon find yourself back at home plate, the same place you started. But now you no longer feel any hurt in your head or heaviness in your heart, only deep peace and a profound feeling of love and compassion. At this point, you know your journey is complete. You appreciate you had to travel far in different directions to find happiness, and understand that this necessarily brought you back to where it all began.

Now, years later, you are better able to understand the journey you undertook. It began at home but you were not aware of who you were or what you were made of. The answers to these questions were there for you to see all the time, of course, but they were hidden from your consciousness by the constant rants and ravings of your ever-critical and dysfunctional mind. Once you went away and progressively removed these impediments, however, you needed only to return home again, where the answers were patiently awaiting your return. With this new awareness and understand-ing—being in this new, enlightened state—you came to see that you also had a new responsibility and calling: To share what you have learned with others for the general betterment of humankind.

> "We have what we seek, it is there all the time, and if we give it
> time, it will make itself known to us."
>
> —Thomas Merton (1915–1968),
> American Trappist Monk, writer, and mystic

Something You Need To Know

Your feelings are always true to your thoughts but your thoughts are not always true to who you are.

Whenever you have an angry thought, it is a lie.

Whenever you have an arrogant thought, it is a lie.

Whenever you have a cruel thought, it is a lie.

Whenever you have a depressing thought, it is a lie.

Whenever you have an envious thought, it is a lie.

Whenever you have a fearful thought, it is a lie.

Whenever you have a greedy thought, it is a lie.

Whenever you have a hateful thought, it is a lie.

Whenever you have a hurtful thought, it is a lie.

Whenever you have an insecure thought, it is a lie.

Whenever you have a jealous thought, it is a lie.

Whenever you have a judgmental thought, it is a lie.

Whenever you have a pretentious thought, it is a lie.

Whenever you have a resentful thought, it is a lie.

Whenever you have a self-deflating thought, it is a lie.

Whenever you have a self-limiting thought, it is a lie.

Whenever you have a selfish thought, it is a lie.

Whenever you have a spiteful thought, it is a lie.

Why? Because this is not who you are!

Some Triumph Over Adversity; Others Do Not

This book is intended to help you wake up and discover your true, authentic Self, and to rejoice and be glad in this knowledge. It follows the printing of my first book, *Think Like A Winner* (Pelican Publishing Company, 1991), available in 14 foreign languages in more than 45 countries around the world. If you google my full name, it shows about 500,000 hits, many of them because of this first book. Needless to say, I am pleased with this result, knowing the book has helped many thousands of people reach new heights of health, wealth, and happiness in both their personal and professional lives.

Now, more than 20 years later, it seems only fitting that I update and expand on the original book, and bring the hope, happiness, and wellness approaches in it up-to-date. The one major advantage I have been able to bring to this process is another 20 years of researching, writing, lecturing, mentoring, and learning. All these activities have been extremely rewarding and joyful, and allow me to share my current understandings and latest insights with you.

Indeed, there are many people in our society today who think like winners and many others who do not. For those who do, however, it may be sporadic, wavering, and unpredictable, as the deep understanding that is required is not understood or fully ingrained. For those who do not, it may be because the considerable emotional pain and suffering they are currently experiencing every day is all they can handle. On both counts, the original book did not offer as detailed and comprehensive an explanation that I know is now possible.

Most people have experienced some pain and suffering in their life. These feelings may have ranged from simple despondency and dejection on occasion to self-doubt, despair, or deep depression, or even to post-traumatic stress disorder (PTSD) and thoughts of suicide. This book is designed to address all these possibilities. The real goal in life is to be positive, peaceful, purposeful, and passionate all the time and always for good reason, and not require any detailed plan or ongoing effort on your part. This is your natural state, and it's only fitting that you should live this way.

Consider a major depressive episode or event as but one example of a significant challenge many people have faced at some point in their life. We all know some very gifted individuals who have suffered from this or a similar malady, yet have managed to find their life purpose and pursue their passion in spite of it. They let both their goodness and greatness define their legacy. As well, we all know many others, also very gifted individuals, who have suffered in the same way and were overwhelmed and totally paralyzed by it. In the latter case, these folks have largely faded into obscurity and are generally unknown to us today. In the former case, a search of the Internet provides the following names of some who have triumphed over this dreaded and potentially debilitating disease:

John Adams (American president)	Drew Carey (comedian/actor)	Ellen DeGeneres (comedian/TV talk show host)
Alan Alda (actor)	Jim Carrey (comedian/actor)	John Denver (singer/songwriter)
Buzz Aldrin (astronaut)	Johnny Cash (singer/songwriter)	Diana, Princess of Wales (British princess)
Woody Allen (film director)	Johnny Carson (TV talk show host)	Charles Dickens (writer)
Hans Christian Andersen (writer)	Dick Cavett (TV talk show host)	Fyodor Dostoyevsky (writer)
Alex Baldwin (actor)	Agatha Christie (crime writer)	Dwight D. Eisenhower (American president)
Roseanne Barr (comedian/actress)	Dick Clark (music personality)	T.S. Eliot (poet)
Drew Barrymore (actress)	John Cleese (actor)	William Faulkner (writer)
Ludwig Von Beethoven (composer)	Ty Cobb (baseball player)	F. Scott Fitzgerald (writer)
Monachem Begin (Israeli prime minister)	Leonard Cohen (singer/songwriter)	Harrison Ford (actor)
Ingmar Bergman (film director)	Joseph Conrad (writer)	Connie Francis (singer)
William Blake (poet)	Calvin Coolidge (American president)	J. Paul Getty (philanthropist)
Terry Bradshaw (football player/TV commentator)	Sheryl Crow (singer/songwriter)	Graham Greene (writer)
Art Buchwald (humorist/writer)	Winston Churchill (British prime minister)	Vincent Van Gogh (painter)
Lord Byron (writer)	Rodney Dangerfield (comedian/actor)	Stephen Hawking (physicist)

Ernest Hemingway (writer)	Marilyn Monroe (actress)	Joan Rivers (comedian)
William James (psychologist)	Claude Monet (painter)	John D. Rockefeller (industrialist)
Billy Joel (singer/songwriter)	Wolfgang Amadeus Mozart (composer)	J.K. Rowling (writer)
Olivia Newton-John (singer/actress)	Rosie O'Donnell (comedian)	Monica Seles (tennis player)
Elton John (singer/songwriter)	Ozzie Osborne (singer)	Rod Steiger (actor)
Samuel Johnson (poet)	Ilie Nastase (tennis player/coach)	James Taylor (singer/songwriter)
John Keats (poet)	Sir Isaac Newton (physicist)	Leo Tolstoy (writer)
Yves Saint Laurent (clothing designer)	Friedrich Nietzche (philosopher)	Mark Twain (writer)
John Lennon (singer/songwriter)	Robert Oppenheimer (physicist)	Mike Wallace (journalist)
Abraham Lincoln (American president)	Marie Osmond (singer)	Walt Whitman (writer)
Martin Luther (theologian)	Gwyneth Paltrow (actress)	Robin Williams (comedian/actor)
Guy de Maupassant (writer)	Jane Pauley (TV anchor)	Tennessee Williams (writer)
Herman Melville (novelist/poet)	T. Boone Pickens (industrialist)	Owen Wilson (actor)
Michelangelo (painter/sculptor)	Edgar Allen Poe (poet/writer)	Virginia Woolf (writer)
John Stewart Mill (political philosopher)	Charlie Pride (singer)	Boris Yeltsin (Russian president)

In some cases, the individuals themselves may not have conquered their malady per se, but rather learned how to live with it and succeed in spite of it. This in itself is most commendable. With recent breakthroughs in various branches of psychology, however, an even more aggressive and permanent approach is now possible. As a result of research findings that are based on extensive clinical trials, many new, very powerful (and drug-free) tools are available today to anyone with similar challenges who wishes to learn about them and apply them in a consistent and concerted way.

As explained, this book describes three specific approaches that deal directly with fear, hurt, anger, guilt, and regret—indeed any negative emotion that is affecting your mood and usurping your energy, thus preventing you from taking positive, purposeful action. It allows the reader to think in new directions, see new possibilities, aim higher, and think bigger and better.

The good news is that help is now available to anyone who is willing to seek it out; the bad news is that no one has an excuse anymore to not develop his or her full potential. The critical path has been laid out for you. You need only move onward, upward, and inward. All that remains is your answer to this key question: Are you willing to accept full responsibility for the way your life will continue to unfold, knowing there will be both ups and downs? Note that your responsibility cited here does not refer to getting *all* ups and absolutely *no* downs; that's just not possible. Rather it refers to how well you are able to deal with the inevitable downs that will occur, and move on in life with unshakeable confidence and courage in spite of them.

The human mind has no limits, it has no boundaries, but you need to push yourself if you're ever to discover who you really are and what you're really made of—if you're ever to unlock the power that lies within.

You Are on a Train That Is Out of Control

"People say that what we're all seeking is a meaning for life. I don't think that's what we are really seeking. I think what we're seeking is an experience of being alive, so that our life experiences on the purely physical plane will have resonances within our own innermost Being and reality, so that we actually feel the rapture of being alive...."

—Joseph Campbell (1904–1987),
American mythologist, writer, and lecturer;
author of *The Masks of God* (1959)

The following describes everyone who has ever lived on the planet or is still clinging to life today, however precariously.

At the physical level, we are all on a path, quite a similar path, in fact. It is one where everything is rapidly changing—absolutely everything! To what end, no one is quite sure, but we do know a lot of suffering is taking place. Yet the exercise cannot be stopped, altered, or interrupted for any significant period of time. It's like a locomotive on a set of tracks that is plowing straight ahead at full speed. We are all passengers on board, being taken for a ride. Best hold on tight! To fall off may well be fatal.

There is much evidence of this constant, incessant, unrelenting change that is taking place. On a personal level, I could say, "Ma'am, did you know a new wrinkle just appeared around the corners of your eyes?" Or, "You, sir, you just lost another hair follicle from the top of your head. That's 10 this week!" Me? I just got a little shorter, my back a little more arched, and my skin a little less taunt. There is much more that is happening all around me, of course, but it is all only an unnecessary distraction. I choose to focus on what is *not* changing—indeed what is permanent and therefore real.

This, then, is the alternative to the arduous, rigid, physical path. As the metaphysical, spiritual, or transcendent level or state of mind, it is "pure" consciousness. It's there all the time, of course, patiently waiting to be noticed. Alas, most people don't see it, understand it, or make use of it. It's when you are *not thinking,* when no thoughts are being generated (at least not by you) and nothing, absolutely nothing, ever changes. It just is.

So when are you in this "passive" mental state? It's when you see, hear, or smell something, then spend a second or two to recognize, accept, and compartmentalize it. It's when you look at a bird, a flower, or a tree, and are overwhelmed for a few seconds with its innate, awesome beauty. It's when you are shocked in the extreme, and it takes a second or two to collect your thoughts about what has just happened. Or it's when you enter Presence, that place of stillness, tranquility, and deep peace, and simply be.

Try it yourself. Enter Presence, and become one with stillness. Do this at 9 a.m., 10 a.m., 11 a.m., or noon today. In each and every case, in that place, you will notice that nothing is changing and no time is elapsing. Stillness knows no form and is never changing. Again, it just is. If you look at your watch in stillness to see what time it is, it will simply say, "Now." And it will always say Now, no matter which day, month, or year you do it, whether this year, next year, or 10 or 20 years from today.

Here, you are not thinking at all. No thoughts. No reactions. No hopes or fears. (This is known as thoughtful thoughtlessness.) You simply *notice* what your body is feeling and your active mind is doing including (among other things) thinking, comparing, judging, and condemning. But as you watch all this activity going on, you realize this is not who you are. Instead, you see you are the greater *knowing* or intelligence that is aware of it. In other words, you are not what is happening; rather you are the space in conscious awareness in which everything is happening!

When you access stillness on a regular, daily basis—whether for five or 25 minutes—it allows you to be more creative, alert and focused, empathetic and ethical, responsible and resilient, and open and welcoming to new ideas, new understandings, and new possibilities. As a result, you will find yourself no longer just clinging to life but more understanding and accepting of life—indeed *celebrating* life, one that involves more hope, more peace, more joy, more happiness, more tolerance, more compassion, and more love.

When you optimize the way you use your mind—both the "active" and "passive" modes—you are engaging in "peak" thinking.

When such thinking is fully mastered, a seemingly impenetrable wall of sadness, confusion, and uncertainty collapses and disappears.

A new world presents itself; the door is open wide.

It is a world of possibility and opportunity, of excitement and discovery.

The experience of being fully aware and fully alive is now available to you.

You need only enter and occupy that space.

Assessing Your Current State of Well-Being (Annex 1)

Consider the following questions to determine your current state of well-being:

1. What percent of the population do you think are living the kind of life they really want (0, 5, 10, 15, 20...)? **How about you**—percent of time each day?

2. What percent of the population do you think are authentically happy? **How about you**—percent of time each day?

3. What percent of the population do you think have the kind of intimate, loving relationships they deeply want? **How about you**—percent of time each day?

4. What percent of the population do you think feel personally fulfilled and immensely satisfied with their life? **How about you**—percent of time each day?

5. What percent of the population do you think are totally at peace with themselves and their world? **How about you**—percent of time each day?

6. What percent of the population do you think feel their life has real meaning and a sense of purpose? **How about you**—percent of time each day?

7. What percent of the population do you think feel they are in complete control of every aspect of their life? **How about you**—percent of time each day?

8. What percent of the population do you think feel a real sense of excitement and exhilaration in their life? **How about you**—percent of time each day?

9. What percent of the population do you think experience serenity, inner joy, and bliss every day of their life? **How about you**—percent of time each day?

10. What percent of the population do you think feel fully engaged, alive, and in constant wonderment and awe? **How about you**—percent of time each day?

So, with the ego removed from the process, what is your score out of 1,000 regarding **"How about you?"** What does this tell you? Do you want to improve your score? Do you know how to improve your score? (Knowing the title of this book, are you surprised that my own score is about 950, or 95 percent?) Regardless of your score, it is my sincere belief that the teachings in this book will increase your score dramatically in each of these areas and to a level you never thought possible. The source of peace, hope, happiness, and love lies deep within you; you need only go there and unite with it to benefit from its phenomenal powers.

Determining Your Level of Authentic Happiness
(Annex 2)

I deeply love and respect myself just as I am.

A (% before)				B (% after)
100	| |	**Unity Consciousness (awake)**	| |	100
90	| |		| |	90
80	| |		| |	80
70	| |		| |	70
60	| |		| |	60
50	| |		| |	50
40	| |		| |	40
30	| |		| |	30
20	| |		| |	20
10	| |	**Unconsciousness (asleep)**	| |	10
0	| |		| |	0

As you begin reading this book, estimate what you think your level of authentic happiness and spiritual awareness is in column A. Then, after having completed it, return to this chart and estimate what you think your level of spiritual awareness is in column B. The difference between the two is an attempt, however simplistic, to measure how much this learning experience was able to help you move ahead toward understanding and enlightenment, as well as how much further you need to go to reach Unity Consciousness. Remember: Just getting out of unconsciousness itself is a great beginning. "A walk of a thousand miles begins with a single step," an ancient Chinese proverb says. I trust the information in this book will be the beginning of many steps you will be taking along the path to Being through awakening to what is.

Ridding Yourself of an Old, Worn-Out Story (Annex 3)
Consider the following:

> "I am in between stories. The old one is gone, and the new one is just beginning to take shape. When we already have a story we are heavily identified with, whether we appear to like this story or not, it is difficult to stay awake, to watch our thoughts and feelings without letting them dictate our actions. A clear story about who we are makes it hard to wait and let our actions arise from the deep and open emptiness of experiencing who we are right now, makes it difficult to allow actions to arise that may be inconsistent with how our story says we should move."

> —Oriah Mountain Dreamer,
> Canadian author of *The Invitation* (1999)

As you pass through life, you come to see yourself as being a certain kind of person who thinks, believes, and acts in certain ways. Your dance, so to speak, has become habitual. Sometimes you are pleased with your behavior; at other times you are not. It seems you are always transitioning from an old, unwanted story to a new, more desirable one and wonder if this will ever end. In this regard, do you consider yourself to be a virtuous person? If so, are you *always* virtuous, or only when the circumstances are appropriate and the timing convenient?

The transition to more virtuous behavior may look something like this:

Sometimes or Always	Kind
Sometimes or Always	Generous
Sometimes or Always	Helpful
Sometimes or Always	Loving
Sometimes or Always	Grateful
Sometimes or Always	Compassionate
Sometimes or Always	Empathetic
Sometimes or Always	Curious
Sometimes or Always	Truthful
Sometimes or Always	Honest
Sometimes or Always	Forgiving
Sometimes or Always	Respectful

And so on.

To note: If who you think you are causes you to constantly flip back and forth like this as you live your life, then I submit you really don't know who you are at all. You are in a sort of no-man's land and making it up as you go along.

This particular list of character traits is not as important as the fact that you clearly identify with them; in fact, you'd like them to define you as a person—as who and what you are. So if you have ended up thinking you are not a kind, loving, and generous person, and hence not worthy and deserving of happiness and love in return, you need to understand that this mind-set is preventing you from breaking free from your past and moving on to explore your true Nature (i.e., always virtuous). Being virtuous only occasionally, when it's convenient, is not the standard you are trying to set.

Preparing for the Journey

Can you imagine being authentically happy almost all of the time, regardless of your circumstances and what is happening in the world? Would not this be as close to heaven on earth that you could find?

This book aims to *inform* and *transform*:

Inform in the sense that it shows you the way the mind/body actually works.

Transform in the sense that it shows you who and what you really are.

You Are "It" and "It" Is You

Think of God as the ocean.

We know an ocean is vast; it is life-enriching; it is powerful and magnificent beyond measure.

Now consider yourself to be a cup from that very same ocean.

Now you too are vast; you, too, are life-enriching; you, too, are powerful and magnificent beyond measure.

Why? Because you are "it" and "it" is you.

Your essence and its essence are exactly the same.

You both are made of the same immaculate "stuff," and that stuff is called love.

Key Concepts We Will Be Exploring Together

On Being

Being defies simple words and description. It can only be experienced. This much can be said: Being is feeling the ever-present I am, of knowing at a higher level of consciousness that you are. This is the state of enlightenment, meaning being free of the illusion of the egoic (little) self, of believing you are nothing more than your physical body and the thoughts you think. It is only through Being that you can connect with your Source, your true essence, that which lies at the very center of all that is.

On Insight

Insight means the ability to see into and understand clearly the nature of a thing or things. In this book, this is what is attempted—to gain insight into the nature of humankind as well as the nature of the Universe through the intellect and intuition. The former is when you analyze information critically, rationally, and logically; the latter is what resonates with your soul and simply feels right. You are encouraged to conduct this same test on the information presented here. Some of it you may connect with, some of it you may not, and that's fine. Just spending time thinking about such ideas has to be considered progress, however. It's something we all need to do if we want to wake up.

On Who You Are

You exist as 99 percent pure fiction, not fact. The Creator had the most important say in who you are, of course, but the rest is a story you yourself compose. How can this be? During your upbringing, you took in a vast amount of *subjective* information: the country, state, city, or town you were born in, who your parents, teachers, and mentors were, your language, religion, traditions, customs, education, and so on. As you began to accept and believe all this information, you turned it into *objective* fact and said, "Good! Now I know who I am!" The result is unfortunate and tragic, however, for by adopting a self-concept or identity that is necessarily limiting, inaccurate, and totally false, you end up living a lie! You never grasp the true Nature of your self—your actual Being.

On Your Emotions

The vast majority of your emotions are contrived. You generate them yourself, continuously and relentlessly, in response to everyday events— whether it is impatience, indifference, intolerance, anger, hate, fear, greed, hurt, guilt, jealousy, envy, or regret. This occurs as you proceed to judge and pre-judge (aka prejudice) the world, and every one and every thing in it using your faulty perceptual artifacts and limited mental capabilities. However, there is one emotion that is always available to you to offset and question your (often-illogical) beliefs and (generally distorted) view of the world: *It is unconditional love.* Yet in this you play no active part. This emotion, if allowed to (i.e., it is not blocked by the ego), comes forth naturally and effortlessly—indeed spontaneously—and from a place you don't fully understand, appreciate, or have any control over. It is the primary characteristic of your Source; it is the essence of your Being; it is who and what you are.

An Explanation of Some Key Terms

"That which does the seeing, cannot be seen; that which does the hearing, cannot be heard; and that which does the thinking, cannot be thought."

—The Vedas (1500–500 BCE),
ancient sacred texts originating in India

1. What is meant by the term "Source"?

Your Source is not an object, a person, or a thing. It is an all-encompassing, all-pervasive *Presence*. It is an energy, a power, an intelligence; it is everywhere and it is good! It is who you are, your essence, your true and only Self. It is that unknowable and indefinable abstraction that lies at the core of all creation. Most simply stated, perhaps, it is that which provokes wonderment and awe. Several names throughout history have been given to this entity that some call God. Others still call it Abba, Adonai, Allah, Almighty, Brahman, Creator, Divine Presence, Great Spirit, Holy One, Infinite Being, Jehovah, Kali, Krishna, One Consciousness, Ra, Source, Supreme Being, Tao, Transcendent Entity, Yahweh, and many other names. You can call it Rachel or Ralph if you like. It doesn't matter what you call it, label it, or conceive it to be; it is what it is.

2. What is the "ego"?

The ego is a derived sense of self, a notion or impression buried deep in your mind that represents who you think you are. It is the ego in you that often says to others, "I'm different from you. I'm separate from you. I'm more important, more deserving, more capable.... Indeed, I'm 'better' than you." It's the result of a belief system that our species has created over the long course of human history because of its need to survive. Primitive man lived in a cruel, rough, and dangerous environment, and survival was his first order of business. Wild animals, other hostile tribes, and a harsh climate all conspired together to put him at risk. This instinct continues to drive the human species today even though many of the threats that existed in earlier times disappeared a long time ago.

3. What is "real"?

Great thinkers throughout history have grappled with this question, and many have come to agree on the following: *That which is real never changes.* So think about it: What is it about you and your world that doesn't change? We know that everything in the visible world, the world of form, changes. Each and every object has a beginning and an end, a birth and a death. This necessarily includes your own physicality—your body. It shrinks, dies, and decays, and becomes the simple dust that makes up our flower beds, lawns, and local parks. Hence, by definition, your body is not real; your body is not the real you. This begs the question: If you are not your physical body, who and what are you?

4. What does it mean to live "authentically"?

Your Source is real, your Source is love, your Source knows only good, your Source is you. If you want to *be* love and *give* love, *be* good and *do* good, you need to align yourself with your Source. You must be it, for it is you. A peaceful mind begins with a caring heart. When you know what your Source is, understand that you are your Source, and then align yourself with this Source in everything you think, say, and do, you can honestly proclaim to the world, "I see only perfection in every aspect of my life." This is what it means to live authentically.

5. Why are nature and the environment so important?

Humankind, from the earliest of civilizations to Native Americans to many environmentalists today, has held a firm and fundamental belief that there is a close and loving relationship between the Father and Mother earth, between God and nature. It holds that to harm the land and fruits of the land is to harm God and, in turn, ourselves. After all, we are all One. Indeed, we have much to learn from nature by simply watching the many processes and practices it puts on display for us to witness, admire, and emulate: acceptance, adaptability, accommodation, nobility, creativity, symmetry, beauty, resourcefulness, regularity, majesty, respect, diversity, freedom, vitality, tolerance, warmth, humility, renewal, interdependence, patience, gratitude, resilience, and determination.

6. What is meant by "Being?"

Don't try to understand Being with your mind; accept only that you need to experience it for yourself. The closest thing in this world to God is silence. Being is experiencing Oneness when in that place called no-mind. It is the state of consciousness that is achieved by going into silence and being still. Being involves living in the moment, in Now, being totally present in the present, and experiencing deep peace and tranquility in that space. You move from a state of conditioned consciousness, meaning consumed by mind (i.e., all the thoughts that the mind generates), to a state of unconditioned consciousness, meaning a place of no-mind (i.e., no thoughts, no ego, no expectations, no judgment).

Equally, it involves a particular kind of mindfulness whereby you direct your attention to a place where there are no thoughts, no distractions, and no concerns—only stillness and solitude. Through this approach, you enter a transformed mental state, and in turn have a transformed experience that is absent of all noise and other unnecessary distractions. By Being, you are able to understand the truth about yourself beyond mind and the world of form. The process is quite simple, in fact: Just allow *what is,* at any instant in time, *to be* in all the fullness and richness that Being is.

7. What is meant by the term the "Now"?

The Now recognizes that there is no past and no future; in fact, no physical or measurable "time" at all. There is only Now, the actual and ever-present moment at hand. Time, our fixation on what we call the past, the present, or the future, is simply an artificial mechanism we humans have created to better manage and control our activities and measure our progress.

The Now is a never-ending, ever-expanding "space" of unimaginable and incalculable proportions, and not a linear line that comes from one direction (past) and heads off in another (future). It is both the *only* point in time and *every* point in time. In fact, it is eternity, which is independent of time. You can live your life only in this one instant: in Now. You cannot think at any point other than in this instant, never have, and never will.

Of course, you can recall a memory from the past but only in the present; and you can imagine or think about the future, but again only in the present. When the future does come, it can come only in the present—in Now. In other words, everything that has ever happened to you in the past happened in Now and everything that will ever happen to you in the future will happen in Now. The only true reality, then, is Now. It's all there is. Equally important, it is also the primary door or portal that allows you to access that place called no-mind. It is through Being in Now, in stillness, in no-mind, that you will find your true and only Self.

8a. What is "mind-ful-ness," as opposed to "mind-less-ness"?

Mindfulness simply involves paying close attention in order to be more aware. It means being present, in the moment, in a non-judgmental way. You can practice mindfulness while doing such things as walking, talking, listening, eating, observing, exercising, thinking, writing, reading, and so forth. To be mindful requires a close, symbiotic relationship between mind and body. Instead of acting habitually, unconsciously, or impulsively, you practice acute, alert awareness regarding the task at hand. You focus; you concentrate; you avoid any and all distractions.

8b. What is "mindfulness meditation" and what role does it play?

Mindfulness meditation can be defined as opening and surrendering to the present moment—Now—with full attention and alert awareness. It involves calming the mind and entering that space called no-mind. It's basically an introspection and contemplation exercise that takes you from "active" thinking into Presence. There are literally hundreds of ways of meditating that have been developed by various spiritual teachers over the past several thousand years, some very formal and others quite informal. You can calm the mind by using relatively simple meditative practices; you don't have to follow a complicated ritual. In fact, if the process is too complicated, it can get in the way of the goal itself—calming the mind.

Calming the mind can be achieved in several ways: (a) by choosing to have no thoughts, not through any strenuous effort on your part but simply by surrendering to what is in Now; (b) by practicing intense, protracted awareness in the present moment by looking at a flower, a bird, a tree, a mountain, or the ocean, and mindfully marveling at its incredible beauty—its actual Being; and (c) by focusing the mind on one or more present moment, bodily related functions such as your breathing, your heartbeat, or the temperature at the very tip of your right big toe.

Alternately, if you just want to divert your attention away from the cascade of compulsive, ever-present, and often-unsettling thoughts you experience all the time, consider imagining what your eyes would see if they were turned around and looking back inside your head! Anything that takes you away from all the noise and preoccupations of your mind (and in the process, both the trivia and trauma of your everyday life) and into a place of stillness and solitude, will have a beneficial effect. (Note: The seven steps to practice mindfulness meditation are listed on page 142.)

9. What is meant by the term "object" consciousness?

"Object" consciousness refers to the manifested world, the world of form, of physicality, of all the objects you are able to perceive through one or more of your five physical senses. If you look around, this in fact is all you will see. There is no end to all the things in your world, and they serve you to the extent that you need or want them. A problem arises, however, if you identify yourself completely and unwittingly with these very same things. Your story could go something like this: "I am my house, my car, my jewelry..." (or any or all of your various possessions). As well, "object" consciousness refers to the mind and all the irrational thoughts, petty concerns, and silly notions (i.e., untruths) that are generated by the mind.

Thoughts are very much *things,* and too many of them can overload your circuits and cause a mental breakdown or burnout. Constant, compulsive thinking with no pause for reflection and rejuvenation is not good for your physical and mental health, nor is it the best use of your mind. All too often people believe they have to think a great deal in order to achieve what they want to achieve, not realizing this is actually not the case. When you are not thinking up a storm is when you are the most alert, the most creative, the most insightful, and certainly the most at peace.

10. What is meant by the term "space" consciousness?

"Space" consciousness refers to the un-manifested world, the world of no-form, of no-thoughts, of no-mind, of no-sound, of no-thing, of silence. If you look up into the sky on a clear, moonlit night, you will see the odd flickering light here and there, and a whole lot of space. Most people tend to focus on the objects they see in space, wondering what they are, but forget about the enormity of space in outer space itself. Perhaps this is because they think such space is just empty and has no meaning or relevance. Ironically, every single object in the physical world is also made up mostly of empty space—more than 95 percent in fact—including your physical body.

Space is very important, because it's by far the major ingredient in everything that exists in both the physical world and the mental domain. As well, you need to realize that a certain complexity arises when you try to describe what is the real nature of space, of emptiness (aka fullness!), of what is seemingly no-thing or nothing. You must be careful not to label it as this or that, however, because then you will understand it only in terms of being this or that. Rather, you should simply accept it as representing the great un-manifested, the substance of no-form, the essence of all creation. Needless to say, you will always remain ignorant of the true nature of "space" consciousness, for "object" consciousness—the thoughts that are generated by your mind—is unable to understand the vastness and depth of the whole Universe. This dimension is simply beyond the ability of your mind to comprehend.

11. Where will my search for my "Self" ultimately take me?

First, don't look upon this as a search. To do so implies you have to work hard at the process and have a specific end in mind; invariably, you will also have certain preconceived expectations about that end. A simple, calm, and open-minded approach is more appropriate and more effective. All that is necessary to begin is a *small, gentle shift* in your attention away from thinking you are someone, from having a compulsive need to be someone, to just Being.

Part of this is realizing that all things are interconnected and inter-related—that Being in fact equals inter-Being. This means understanding and accepting that every thing on the planet, including every creature, every object, and every individual, is made up of the same basic ingredients or elements that are found in our physical world (i.e., hydrogen, nitrogen, oxygen, carbon, iron, magnesium, lead, silver, selenium, chromium, lithium, etc.). In this sense, when you look at a rock, a flower, a tree, a bird, an animal, or another human being, you are in fact looking at your Self. In the same way, when you show love, concern, and respect toward any of these same things, you are showing love, concern, and respect for your Self. *In this sense, all love is self-love.* The result is a "we versus me" mentality or mind-set, a sense or *knowing* that we are not all separate entities, creatures, or organisms, and therefore need special and individual treatment. We are all One. We are all made from the same basic ingredients of One-ness.

12. Can you recommend certain individuals or teachings for further study?

If you wish to conduct research on your own into the topic of practical spirituality, here are the names of some noted religious figures and spiritual masters:

Abraham (c. 2000 BCE), who is widely regarded as the patriarch of Jews, Christians, and Muslims. The Covenant between God and Abraham forms the basis for Judaism, and is considered to be the first or one of the first monotheistic religions.

Buddha, which literally means "the awakened one," whose teachings form the basis of Buddhism. Buddhism is based on the life of Siddharta Gautama (c. 563–c. 483 BCE), an Indian prince.

Lao-tzu (c. 604–531 BCE), author of the definitive book *Tao Te Ching* and founder of Taoism.

Adi Shankaracharya (788–820 CE), the first person to consolidate the key principles of Advaita Vedanta, which is a Hindu philosophy that believes in the indivisibility of the Self and the Whole.

Jesus Christ (c. 3 BCE–30 CE), a Jew born in Palestine whose life and teachings form the basis of Christianity. There are many denominations of Christianity, the two main ones being Orthodox and Western Christianity.

Mohammed (570–632 CE), also spelled Muhammad, the founder of Islam, considered by Muslims to be the last messenger and prophet of God. Mohammed claimed to be a messenger of God in the same vein as Adam, Noah, Moses, David, Jesus, and other notable prophets.

What kind of God would create imperfect Beings and interact with them from a distance?

How to Live the Enlightened Life

"Man has falsely identified himself with the pseudo-soul or ego. When he transfers his sense of identity to his true Being, the immortal soul, he discovers that all pain is unreal. He can no longer even imagine the state of suffering."

—Paramahansa Yogananda (1893–1952,
Indian spiritual teacher,
author of *Autobiography of a Yogi* (1946)

It all begins with the erroneous notion of separation—the idea that there is a you and there is a me, that you have your physical body and I have mine, that you are there and I am here, that you have your space and I have mine, that you are alone and I am alone. This can be extended to mean I must look after and protect myself and my interests, knowing that you will try to look after and protect yourself and your interests; that I want to survive, prosper, and succeed just as you want to survive, prosper, and succeed.

But each of us believes there is only so much to be had or so it appears in the physical world. (After all, a pizza has only so many slices!) The things I want are also the things you want, which means I have to compete with you to make sure I get what I want at the expense of you getting what you want. This can only lead to confrontation and conflict, to winning and losing. Look around and you will see just how much of this is going on in our world today whether between individuals, various ethnic, tribal or religious groups, or indeed whole nations.

As Eckhart Tolle, author of *The Power of Now* (1997), has explained, there have probably been times in your life when things didn't go as you had hoped. As happened to him, this may have prompted you to mutter such statements as "I'm not happy with myself," "I hate myself," or "I can't live with myself anymore." This is what people often say to themselves when they are down and depressed, and may even be having suicidal thoughts. At this point, however, a fortunate few have noticed a strange duality in their internal discourse. They wonder and ask themselves, "When I say, 'I-am-not-happy-with-my-self,' I seem to be talking about two people or entities at play here, first an 'I' as well as a 'self.' So who is this 'I' and what is this 'self,' anyway?"

A good question! As has been explained, there are indeed two entities at play in your mind. One is your Source, your true identity, your eternal essence, the knower—often referred to as God, the Source, or the Infinite. The other is the ego, your false self, the constant thinker, your tormentor, the great pretender, your so-called "little self."

Your inner dialogue, then, is saying, "The 'I' in me that is my true Self, is sick and tired of putting up with you, the other 'self,' my false self, that part of me that is forcing me to think that I am separate, I am alone, I am vulnerable. Yes, I'm very tired of living out this charade. It's not the real me that is living my life this way. This way, I don't experience any joy, any fulfillment; there is no peace, no love. It's so draining, so stressful, so depressing. It's all so unproductive. There must be a better way, a way out of all this silliness, all this nonsense, all this insanity."

The ego in us is something we ourselves created during the long course of human history as a survival mechanism. Primitive man had to cope with other hostile tribes, a harsh environment, and marauding, vicious animals looking for a quick meal. Man necessarily had to develop ways to protect himself, to survive these elements and constant threats. It basically came down to the fight-or-flight response: Engage the enemy and kill it any way you can, or run as fast as you can and hopefully escape to come back and fight another day.

And so the ego was "born." We created it, we did it all by ourselves, and in a very real sense we did it *to* ourselves. And we have been living with it ever since, even though many of the threats of these earlier times no longer exist. In most cases, we have tamed the environment and brought wild animals under our control, but have yet to stop seeing enemies—other human beings!—all around us.

So here is the reality. First, those with the biggest egos and who were willing to take the most extreme measures were the ones who survived. And second, because they did survive, you and I descended from them; we inherited their DNA. We are them in their most recent incarnation, complete with all their vanity, arrogance, greed, cruelty, and neuroses. To note, the more peace-loving Neanderthals were killed off by the more aggressive Cro-Magnons about 30,000 years ago (Source: Wikipedia).

Imagine prehistoric man acting totally in his own self-interest as he says to his fellow hunter-gatherers, "See that water buffalo over there? That's my water buffalo. Stay away from it. I want that water buffalo to feed myself and my family. My family and I are more important than you and your family. We intend to survive and I really don't care what happens to you. If you try to take that water buffalo away from me, I'll stop you any way I can: I'll trick you, I'll steal from you; in fact, I'll fight you to the death for it. I'll do whatever it takes to keep that water buffalo!"

The ego, pure and simple, is a figment of our imagination. It's an illusion, a mental construct or fabrication; it's something we use to supposedly protect ourselves and further what we deem to be in our self-interest, including our survival. The ego, acting on our behalf, says to others: "I'm more important than you," "I'm 'better' than you," "I'm more deserving than you," "I'm right; you're wrong," "I need to win (and in the process make sure you lose)," and so on. The ego wants you to think of it as your great protector and benefactor when in fact it is not. It only wants to control you to further its own agenda, which it does by controlling the thoughts you think from minute-to-minute and day-to-day.

By controlling your thoughts, which invariably focus on either what you desire or what you fear, the ego is able to control your emotions and in turn the actions you take on a daily basis. In effect, you become it because it is being you; it is making you do what it wants you to do, pretending it has your best interests in mind.

When the ego is at work in your mind, saying all the things we have said it says ("I'm this and I'm that," etc., etc.), all at the expense of other people, this collectively is called noise or mental turbulence. The ego is a noise generator of monumental proportions. Noise suits the purposes of the ego very well: It distracts, it distorts, it corrupts, and it weakens the person in whom it resides and thus prevents you from knowing your Source—your true identity.

The greatest fear of the ego is that you will discover the charade it is perpetrating on you and how you see yourself, for if you turn down all the noise that the ego creates, with its misguided musings and selfish mutterings, you will find yourself going more and more into silence. Silence to the ego is the ultimate killer, for that is where you will find your Source. And once you find your Source, there is nothing left for the ego to do. Its constant chatter will slowly dissipate and its power over you will begin to subside. Although it is practically impossible to reduce the ego in you to absolutely zero, you can reduce it to an insignificant shadow of its former self.

The ego doesn't want to be marginalized in any way, so it operates in constant survival mode. It will go to any extreme to ensure that this doesn't happen, even to the point of having you kill yourself, which will result in its own death as well (i.e., just as cancer itself dies when it kills someone). No matter the cost, it will fight the good fight to the bitter end.

So the battle rages on. It's a real war and one that takes place in your mind moment-by-moment, day-after-day, thought-by-thought-by-thought. Today, looking at all the carnage that is going on in the world, the ego is winning on many fronts but thankfully not on all. I like the wisdom contained in this comment: *We—individually—have to mend our mind before we—collectively—can mend the world.*

Consider human consciousness and the choices that are available to you. To begin, you need to understand that everything in fact happens in Now. For example, you can think about the past, the present, or the future, but only in Now. In other words, you cannot think about the past in the past or about the future in the future, for neither the past nor the future exists other than as thoughts that you entertain in Now.

Because you cannot think anywhere other than in Now, the Now is all there is. It's filled with ongoing, constantly flowing, ever-present thoughts. If you carefully analyze what kinds of thoughts dominate your everyday thinking, you will find that the vast majority them—more than 95 percent in some people—are egoic (i.e., ego-based/ego-generated thoughts). Examples include (although perhaps a little on the extreme side):

"Poor me."

"I don't deserve to live like this."

"I don't deserve to be treated like this."

"I don't deserve to be so miserable, so poor, so sad, so unpopular, so unattractive, so unlucky."

"I deserve *more*—more of this and more of this and more of this!"

These, then, are the messages you shout out to the world, asking it—sorry, demanding of it—to acknowledge and validate your importance, your worthiness, your abilities, your intelligence—your whatever. This is the great noise factor, and as you create it, others create it as well. In fact, the more you create it on your behalf, the more others will create it on their behalf, each side protecting its own turf, meaning their distorted and incomplete sense of self.

Until you understand and see that this is what the ego does—that this is the game it plays, and that it really doesn't care about you—you will not be able to deal with it. The trick is to consciously turn down the noise by recognizing the ego for what it is, then ignoring it to the best of your ability. Necessarily this is quite difficult to do at first. (The ego has been running our minds for a very long time; in fact, for about 1.7 million years and counting!) But with practice, diligence, and a good deal of patience, it soon becomes habit.

The solution? Consider making a friend of stillness several times a day by entering Presence. This is an ideal way to escape from the saddening and often maddening storm that is raging in your mind a good deal of the time. Thankfully, stillness doesn't need to be created, nor is it difficult to find; it already exists, and is everywhere and anywhere you choose to look. It is always welcoming and receptive, and brings a broader perspective to your outlook, as well as joy and jubilation to your heart.

So during your day, perhaps while sipping a sweet-smelling tea, hearing a child's infectious laugh, or watching a tree gently bend in the breeze, try to see what is beyond that—beyond the physical form in which all this is happening. We know that every message sent our way comes with a deeper meaning: First, what we see and think it is, and second, what we don't see and it really is. This is because every aspect of life in the manifested state (i.e., the physical plane) also expresses an aspect of the Divine in the unmanifested state (i.e., the spiritual plane).

Or consider this approach: As the constant flow of ego-based thoughts and concerns impacts your mind and causes you unnecessary anxiety and hurt, go into stillness and simply say, "Please go away. You are of no use to me. You have caused me enough pain and suffering. I have better things to do with my life than listen to you." And you must say this with sincere love as well as firm conviction. Don't try to resist these thoughts or stop them from coming your way with any conscious effort on your part. That only gives them power. Just let them know that you don't want to hear them anymore. The welcome mat that was once laid at the doorstep of your mind now firmly says, "Go away!"

At this point, slowly but surely, the decibel level of the noise in your mind will begin to subside; you will bask in that place known as stillness and automatically connect with your Source. New understandings and insights emanating from your Source will now impact your inner consciousness, as will their associated emotions that include peace, hope, harmony, joy, beauty, tolerance, compassion, and unconditional love.

Quite a different dynamic follows. Instead of confronting people by judging them, criticizing them, or labeling them in any number of ways, or even attacking them with your anger, you shower them with your kindness and your love, you honor them for their Being, you bestow upon them the respect and dignity that both they and you deserve. You accept them as your equal, you accept them as your brother or sister, and in this way you salute the God in them on behalf of the same God that is in you.

We are not separate from one another, nor are we separate from our Source. To believe otherwise is the cause of all our pain and suffering; to believe otherwise is an illusion, a mistake, a grave error in our thinking.

"We are potentially all things; our personality is what we are able to realize of the infinite wealth which our divine human nature contains deep in its depth."

—William Ralph Inge (1860–1954),
English theologian and Anglican priest,
author of *Light, Life and Love* (1904)

"How is it possible that a being with such sensitive jewels as the eyes, such enchanted musical instruments as the ears, and such a fabulous arabesque of nerves as the brain can experience itself as anything less than a god?"

—Alan Watts (1915–1973),
English writer, thinker, and interpreter of Zen Buddhism,
author of *The Way of Zen* (1957)

"Deep within man dwells those slumbering powers; powers that would astonish him, that he never dreamed of possessing; forces that would revolutionize his life if aroused and put into action."

—Orison Swett Marden (1850–1924),
American writer and philosopher,
author of *He Can Who Thinks He Can* (1908)

Knowing About the Now

What is a "pure" thought, one without ego?

It is a non-thought, a direct experience.

So what is a direct experience?

It's an experience in the moment, in stillness, in Now.

Here you are able to access and come to know "pure," untainted awareness. Here, and only here, you come to know your Self.

**P
A
R
T**

1

"To Think" or "Not to Think," That Is the Question

Accept the present moment—yes, this very instant—fully and unconditionally, and with gratitude. This will put you at ease with your surroundings and connect you to your higher Self.

In Part 1, our focus is on the present moment, the precious present, or Now (all of these terms are interchangeable). The goal is to see how you can use your mind in different ways to get the optimum results.

The Now

In Now, we have seen that you can think about the past, the present, or the future, but in a very real sense the past has never been and the future never will be. Both have happened (the past) or can happen (the future) only in Now. Forget about your past; it happened only to teach you important lessons to better equip you to be in Now. Forget about your future; it will happen by default anyway as you practice Being in the present.

Being—uniting with your eternal essence in the moment—is where all your joy is; it is how you can be fully human and intensely alive. To do otherwise is to only know the ego better, and the ego has nothing to teach you. It has no joy, only pain, to share with you. Its only role is to prevent you from coming to know who and what you are, from discovering your Source. The ego is the great pretender. It wants you to think that you are it and it is you. In fact, its very existence and power over you depend on it.

Knowing Your Options

Let's summarize the different ways you can use your mind. The first is the "active" mode of thinking, the usual cognitive process that involves a series of compulsive, often-repetitive thoughts that you use to get through each day. The second, often misunderstood and seldom used, is the "passive" mode of not thinking that involves going into stillness, into silence, into no-mind. Here, in this relaxed, natural state, the goal is crystal clear: It is to not have any thoughts at all!

The first way you can use your mind, to *think,* is the more common way that involves such activities as perceiving, conceptualizing, rationalizing, and internalizing what you understand and believe is happening at any given moment in time (i.e., what you end up accepting as your current reality). The second, and more important way, involves using your mind to *not think,* which in turn allows you to access inner wisdom that points to truth.

So at any point in time, you can choose to think; this is "object" consciousness, where the mind is fully engaged. Or you can choose to not think, which is "space" consciousness, where the mind is fully disengaged. The ratio for the average person during the course of a day might be 95 percent think and 5 percent not think. The ratio for Tibetan monks, on the other hand, might be the exact opposite: 5 percent think and 95 percent not think. You need only look into the face of a Buddhist monk to see who is most at peace with himself and his world.

Critically, you need to know that there is a third option as well, indeed a more subtle and sophisticated one that combines the best elements of both approaches. In this instance, you choose to engage with, respond to, and be part of everything that is happening all around you, all the while having your mind anchored firmly in the field of conscious Presence or deep peace. Here, instead of being immersed in thought, constrained by thought, or consumed by thought, you retain an element of being in the moment, in Now (i.e., a detached, innocent observer of everything that is happening all around you). This is the ideal way, indeed the optimum way, to use your mind as it incorporates the best of both "worlds" (i.e., form and no-form) that are available to you. This is called mindful living.

"Thinking" in Now

You already are who you really are. Therefore you don't have to expend any effort to create it; you need only access it. This you can do through stillness.

Here are some characteristics concerning *thinking* in Now, in "object" consciousness (this is the "active" mode):

1. Lots of things are happening; thoughts are always being generated.

2. Some things are fine; others are not.

3. Most of your thoughts are goal-oriented (possibilities and probabilities), and almost always driven by the ego.

4. Everything is changing (i.e., things are incomplete and impermanent, always in a state of flux).

5. **There is *always* some suffering going on.**

6. Thinking here is shallow/limited versus deep/unlimited.

This is the confused, corrupted state of "self" consciousness.

"Not Thinking" in Now

Alternately, here are some characteristics concerning *not thinking* in Now, in "space" consciousness (this is the "passive" mode):

1. Nothing is happening; few if any thoughts are being generated.

2. Everything is fine.

3. There is no goal-oriented activity in your mind at all.

4. Nothing changes (i.e., everything is complete and permanent).

5. **There is *never* any suffering going on.**

6. Thinking here is deep/unlimited versus shallow/limited;

7. Through revelation, you come to understand many things about your Self, including your Source—indeed the Oneness of your actual Being. The true meaning of all this resides within you, in universal mind, and can be accessed only through no-mind.

This is the clear, uncorrupted state of "pure" consciousness.

Regarding your ability to think or not think when using your mind, we see there are certain—and indeed very different—benefits that apply to each one. Arguably the most important benefit of all is the fact that when you engage regularly in not thinking, in stillness, *spiritual truths and inner knowings* are unwittingly, anonymously, and spontaneously made known to you; who and what you are, are revealed to you. Hence once you know these aspects of your Being, you have been set free; the thick veil of confusion and illusion has been lifted. You can now think, feel, and act in accordance with your Self, and not in accordance with some incomplete, inaccurate, or distorted version of it.

Exploring the Dimensions of a New Consciousness

> ### FORM
> • the physical domain • known but not real • you can easily see it •
> *everything* is changing • thinking is shallow and limited
> • there is *always* some suffering going on
> • the corrupted state of "self" consciousness

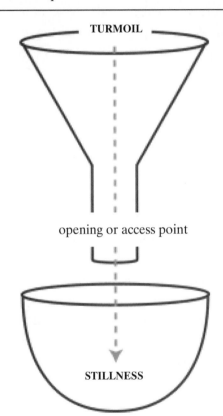

> ### NO FORM
> • the spiritual domain • unknown but real • you cannot see it
> • *nothing* is changing • thinking is deep and unlimited
> • there is *never* any suffering going on
> • the clear state of "pure" consciousness

Figure 1

Because most people spend more than 95 percent of each day actively doing and less than 5 percent actually being, it should be no surprise that they have serious problems. Such people are often over-stressed, over-anxious, and over-stimulated, and prone to bouts of depression and despair on a regular basis. The new term for this affliction is generalized anxiety disorder, or GAD.

So here is the relevant question: Knowing what has just been said about these two different states of mind, why wouldn't you want to spend more time in not thinking, in a place—in fact the *only place*—where you can find the answer to the three critical aspects of your life, namely the answer to these intriguing questions: "Who am I?" "What am I made of?" and "Why am I here?"

It's important to understand how no-mind opens the door to inner peace, tranquility, and enlightenment. It's also key to know the different ways you can enter no-mind and some of the things you will find there. Briefly, you can enter no-mind by personal choice—for example, by taking time to calm the mind through acute attention, keen observation, accepting the present moment, meditation, yoga, tai chi, or some other similar approach. Regarding these options, some may appeal to you more than others or you may find some more effective than others.

Fine. It's only important that you practice whatever you choose on a regular basis. The alternative is not nearly as pleasant, and it's where you have far less control. This is where you are forced to enter no-mind by everyday circumstances—for example, by a major shock or tragedy of one kind or another as a result of a personal life situation or a collective disaster.

Eight Ways to Stop Thinking

Following are eight ways you can calm the mind and get to a place where the ego has minimal or no influence.

When in stillness, you are in the clear state of "pure" awareness. Note that no matter what process you choose to calm the mind, it is relatively simple. Yet to actually do it on a systematic, daily basis is not that easy. Why? You have been living in the world of thought all of your life, so to change takes considerable self-discipline, patience, and persistence, as well as a certain amount of curiosity and courage. Unfortunately, a good number of people are not up to the challenge at their current stage of development.

The eight ways are:

1. **Noticing the short period of time between perceiving something with one of your five senses and assigning a certain meaning or label to it.** There is always a gap—a small instant in time—until you can retrieve from your memory bank an understanding or name for what you are seeing or hearing. This gap, a moment of no-thing-ness or no-mind, offers you a unique opportunity to ponder and reflect before you ultimately respond under control or react out of control.

2. **Noticing the time—the short, silent, yet tangible gap—between your thoughts, or between words in a conversation, or between notes in a musical score, or around letters printed on a page.** Interestingly, any printed page is about 95 percent white space and only 5 percent black ink. These gaps play a key role, as they break up the information that is on display into smaller and more manageable bits. Clearly most of the meaning comes from the so-called "empty" space that surrounds the letters and not from the letters themselves. When you are in a gap, in no-mind, your thinking apparatus is not engaged. Here, nothing is being experienced, nothing is being analyzed, and no decisions are being made. This is a different reality, one where you are free from the constant train of thoughts (an interesting word there: *train!*) that usually consumes your mind, and in turn severely limits your experience and understanding of what is true and what is real.

3. **Experiencing a personal tragedy or disaster, often a major loss of some kind.** It could involve yourself, a friend, or a loved one. Regarding yourself, it could involve finding out that you have a serious illness or becoming aware of your own imminent death.

4. **Experiencing a collective disaster, which again often involves a major loss of some kind.** It could include inhuman conduct involving a mass shooting or suicide, great destruction of property, great loss of life, a natural disaster, or indeed several of these all happening at the same time as a result of a major earthquake, hurricane, tornado, typhoon, flood, or tsunami. Watching the news on TV or reading a daily newspaper tells us that disasters are quite common, both personal and collective. And strange as it may seem, people often find God—or unlimited peace, which is the same thing—as a result of the suffering they witness or experience themselves.

5. **Acute, alert awareness that involves directing your attention to marvel at the essence of some animate/inanimate object such as a rock, a flower, a tree, an animal, or indeed another human being.** This is perceiving without labeling, without thought, without judgment, for once we label something, we think we know it and then cease any further effort to fully understand it. Here, sensory perception involves no thought, no interpretation, and no effort, and doesn't have a past or future. That's why this practice instantly takes you into no-mind.

6. **Focused attention on the present moment.** This involves being present with no story, no thoughts, no preconceptions, and no expectations. This way of having no thoughts doesn't require any effort on your part. You simply allow what is—at any point in time—to be. It's that simple. A question: What would this meditation be like for you if you were sitting in a small, dingy jail cell serving a life sentence...for thinking too much? Of course, most of us are doing just that, but are unaware we are actually imprisoned in a jail and one of our own making!

7. **Informal meditation.** This includes practicing mindfulness regarding various activities such as eating, then carefully chewing every mouthful 15 to 20 times; showering and diligently washing the many parts of your body; walking and being aware of every physical movement you initiate; painting; golfing;

fencing; gardening; fly-fishing; bird-watching; star-gazing—any activity that involves alert, focused attention on a few but important primary tasks.

8. **Formal meditation.** This includes the practice of loving-kindness meditation, which focuses on generating feelings of compassion, warmth, and deep affection for all living things. Similarly, as has been said, it could involve focused attention on some inner body function such as your breathing, as is the case in mindfulness meditation. It could also involve focused attention on a word, a phrase (called a mantra), or an object/building of reverence such as an artifact, a monument, an inscription, or a holy shrine.

Why do these practices work? They work because the mind cannot focus on two things at the same time. It processes all data—thoughts, experiences, and feelings—sequentially. As a test, try laughing and crying at exactly the same time. You cannot. The mind was designed and built to work this way. To note, this is also why we are not very good at multitasking.

If you initiate any of the activities or are subjected to any of the situations just described, the focused attention that results completely fills and occupies your whole mind space, thus preventing the usual flurry of unrelenting, unwanted, and often disturbing thoughts, concerns, and other distractions from entering your consciousness. Clearly, there are several ways you can escape from the daily chaos, turmoil, and confusion that invariably infect your mind. All you need to know is this: what door to open to achieve that end. Then calmly and confidently walk right in!

Have you noticed that every noise or sound that occurs in the world around you—whether it's a person's voice, a truck's engine, a thunder clap, an infant's cry, or a bird's melodic song (or even an annoying or disturbing thought you may have)—always turns into silence at some point? Each is temporary, each exists for a while in the world of form. But every one eventually disappears into silence, into stillness, into the great, welcoming void. This place is permanent. Stillness never changes. It just is and always will be.

Why Is Life So Darn Difficult? (Annex 4)

Life is the investigative tool we use to find truth. Unfortunately, our primary method is trial and error.

The following explains what I have come to believe lies at the core of why so many people have serious problems in their life.

First and foremost, they don't love themselves enough. They therefore go through life trying desperately (and usually unsuccessfully) to fill this huge and unsightly void. As a needy person always wanting something you should already have, namely self-love, you are bound to act in unproductive and dysfunctional ways while relating to others, thus making your life quite miserable and yourself extremely unhappy.

Second, even if a person understands that he doesn't love himself enough and needs to work earnestly and persistently on this key aspect of his personality, it's unlikely this person has any deep insight regarding how to go about it. After all, he has probably never received any special instruction or training in this area (except, perhaps, of a religious kind, which may or may not have been helpful).

The result? His ever-present, self-serving ego jumps in and says, "Hey! Listen to me. I know what you're going through. Just do as I say and everything will turn out fine." If you buy into this desperate and self-serving plea, which appears immensely enticing on the surface, then for sure there is no hope. The ego never has your innermost needs in mind.

We see if these two considerations—a need for self-love and knowing how to get it—are not properly addressed, little of consequence in your life will change, and the usual problems, disappointments, and set-backs will just repeat themselves. Hmmm. A merry-go-round that isn't so merry and is extremely difficult to get off of. But there is a way to get off, as has been explained. As a result, you will find yourself living in a very different world, one that is more inviting, more accepting, and certainly more empowering. The following statement describes in a very succinct and dramatic way what the liberating process is in this regard:

❋───────────────────

Your Source is all loving, all powerful, and all knowing.

It follows that once you understand your Source, identify with your Source and become One with your Source, so, too, will you take on these same attributes.

───────────────────❋

Common Symptoms of Depression (Annex 5)

Depression can affect anyone, at any age, but the risk is highest among those 15 to 24 years old. Estimates are that one in five people will suffer from a major depressive episode at least once in his lifetime. Consider the following list. If you have many or all of the following symptoms on a daily basis, for two weeks or longer, you are likely to be depressed.

* Feeling numb and emotionally drained.

* Having no interest in doing things you previously found enjoyable.

* Experiencing a significant change in appetite, leading to either weight loss or gain.

* Having difficulty thinking, remembering, or focusing on things.

* Wanting to be quiet and alone, away from people/events.

* Feeling stressed, anxious, and generally quite worthless.

* Being tearful; engaging in spontaneous, uncontrolled sobbing or crying.

* Avoiding making decisions, both big and small.

* Having difficulty sleeping or needing too much sleep.

* Believing you have no future/your life is a total waste.

* Having thoughts about death or suicide on a regular basis.

Helpful Websites about Depression

National Institute of Mental Health (U.S.) (*www.nimh.nih.gov*). Provides information about the symptoms of depression, etc.

Mental Health Works (Canada) (*www.menatlhealthworks.ca/facts/*). Provides information about how to maintain mental health throughout one's life, etc.

NHS National Electronic Library for Health (UK) (*www.library.nhs.uk/mentalhealth/*). Answers questions about depression and other mood disorders.

"We need to find God, and he cannot be found in noise and restlessness. God is a friend of silence. See how nature—trees, flowers, grass—grows in silence; see the stars, the moon and the sun, how they move in silence.... We need silence to be able to touch souls."

—Mother Teresa of Calcutta (1910–1997),
Albanian-born Roman Catholic nun,
and founder of Missionaries of Charity;
author of *A Simple Path* (1995)

"If we know the divine art of concentration, if we know the divine art of meditation, if we know the divine art of contemplation, easily and consciously we can unite the inner world and the outer world."

—Sri Chinmoy (1931–2007),
Indian artist, poet, musician, and spiritual teacher;
author of *The Wings of Joy* (1977)

"To learn to be ourselves, we have to start with what we have—and what we always have is our experience in the moment. If we allow ourselves to be in the experience in the moment—to feel it, to see it, to taste it, to hear it, to smell it, to be aware of it—then it becomes possible for us to find out what we are and to be who we are."

—A.H. Almaas (b. 1944),
author of *The Unfolding Now: Realizing Your True Nature
Through the Practice of Presence* (2008)

Knowing How to "Think"

Success in life is an inner game, a state of mind. And each of us can develop our mind but first we must want to do it, then take the time to do it. Unfortunately, not everyone is up to this challenge.

PART

2

Thinking in the Now

In Part 2, we look at how you can *think* in the Now, in the "active" mode of mind. Consider the following:

It is your thoughts that make your life what it is today. It follows that if you change the quality of your thoughts, you will necessarily change the quality of your life.

The primary skill you need to develop when actively thinking in Now is *critical thinking* (CT). This involves noticing, analyzing, and modifying cognitions, assumptions, opinions, and beliefs, with the goal of significantly reducing negative and destructive emotions and subsequent negative and destructive behavior. In the mental health field, this practice is exactly the same and is called *cognitive-behavioral therapy* (CBT). CBT, also known as "talk" therapy, is widely used today to treat various kinds of neurosis and psychopathology, including a wide variety of mood and anxiety disorders.

Regarding both CT and CBT, the process involved requires you to critically question basic assumptions, understandings, and beliefs (i.e., what a person uses to evaluate and internalize a given event and then come to some conclusion about it) that may well be illogical or irrational, or indeed totally inaccurate. The approach follows from Rational Emotive Behavioral Therapy (REBT), which was developed by Albert Ellis (1913–2007) in the 1950s, and further refined by Aaron T. Beck in the 1970s.

Note that we are not talking about positive thinking as the primary solution here, the notion that you must think only happy or positive thoughts all the time. (You could end up in a small, padded cell for doing that!) This high-risk approach—simply being optimistic for the sake of being optimistic—is as dangerous a malady as having only unhappy thoughts all the time.

The following example, perhaps an experience you have had yourself, illustrates what we are talking about. Having failed an important exam, Jack concludes and says to himself, "I'm dumb and useless, and will never get a college degree." This in turn lowers his self-confidence and belief in his abilities, affects his assessment of his future prospects, and even causes him to question his overall self-worth. All this in turn negatively impacts his mood, his level of motivation, his energy, and his belief that he will eventually succeed. Jack begins to study less, pay less attention during lectures, skip classes, argue with his professors, and leave important assignments to the last minute. His behavior is thus confirming his newfound belief: that he is dumb and useless, and will not get that college degree he so desperately wants.

In therapy, this example is called a self-fulfilling prophecy or a problem-pain cycle (i.e., recall the problem, relive the pain). The efforts of the therapist and client are to work together to reassess the particulars of the activating event itself, such as failing an exam, to see if other conclusions are just as plausible/realistic or indeed more plausible/realistic than the one initially adopted. If this systematic-thought-evaluation-process (S-T-E-P) helps the client to think and respond differently, to see that indeed it is possible to draw different conclusions from the same event, then his negative habit pattern of thought can be interrupted and his mood modified so that it is more empowering and productive. As explained, the main objective of CBT is to identify and debunk maladaptive cognitions, assumptions, and beliefs that give rise to debilitating negative emotions that, in turn, can lead to dysfunctional and potentially destructive behavior—in other words, doing harm (physically or emotionally) to oneself or others.

Of note, CBT sessions in some cases can have an immediate and lasting positive impact (i.e., after only a few days or weeks); in other cases, it can take three to six months or even up to a year. All this is understandable, knowing that we are trying to dramatically change an entrenched habit pattern here, in this case one that represents a person's particular manner of thinking.

We know people's core beliefs about themselves and their world are formed, confirmed, and firmly embedded in their psyche during their early childhood years. These then lead to automatic thought responses to everyday events and are not easily overridden. Hence it is only through concerted effort and repetition—applying S-T-E-P over and over again—that new, more productive habit patterns of thought can be generated and over time become the new "norm."

J.K. Rowling, author of the highly successful *Harry Potter* series of books, is a case in point. As a result of selling nearly 400 million books worldwide, she is one of the richest women in Great Britain, with an estimated net worth in excess of $1 billion. However, times were not always so good.

In an interview published on March 23, 2008, on the front page of *The (London) Sunday Times,* she confided that she had thoughts of suicide while suffering from depression as a struggling single mother, after separating from her first husband, a Portuguese TV journalist, in the mid-1990s. "(My) mid-twenties life circumstances were poor and I really plummeted," Rowling, now 49, said. She explained that she sought help from her GP and consequently spent nine months taking cognitive-behavioral therapy. She added that she came out of it feeling fine.

The Times article goes on: "Cognitive-behavioral therapy typically involves a series of sessions with a counselor and is designed to help patients control negative thoughts. The technique is recommended by the (United Kingdom) health department for depressive disorders, anxiety, bulimia, and post-traumatic stress disorder."

Rowling concludes her remarks in the article by saying, "I have never been remotely ashamed of having been depressed. Never. What's to be ashamed of? I went through a really tough time and I am quite proud that I got out of that."

The Process of "Thinking"

Using the example of Jack, the student cited in the previous section, here is a more detailed explanation of the A-B-Cs of the systematic-thought-evaluation-process, which lies at the core of CBT:

> A—**activating event:** This refers to the objective situation or external stimulus—the event, occurrence, or specific incident—that triggers a cognitive response in the first place.

B—cognitive response: This refers to how you interpret and come to some conclusion—thoughts often manifested in the form of self-talk—about that event. This necessarily is a reflection of your personal belief system and the particular habit patterns of thought you have adopted and use instinctively every day.

C—emotional reaction: This refers (as in Jack's case) to the distressing feelings—whether fear, hurt, anger, guilt, or sorrow—that the thoughts in **B** automatically generate. Action (which may be more harmful than helpful) or inaction (inability to decide on a given course of action) immediately follows.

In other words, as you go about your daily routine, *events* (**A**) will invariably occur that cause *thoughts* (**B**) to be generated, which in turn produce *feelings* (**C**) that correspond to these very same thoughts. Now, note the following: The events that occur—in terms of type, frequency, and intensity—are generally out of your control; the thoughts you produce as a result are totally within your control; and the feelings that follow are totally out of your control, as they are a direct result of the particular thoughts that just preceded them. Hence we see where you have to focus your attention if you want to change how you feel:

It is on the thoughts you create in response to various events!

In this regard, most of your responses to situations that arise each day are spontaneous and automatic; they are primarily habitual, meaning you don't give them any serious (conscious) consideration before they appear. But if you want, you can learn to change how you respond to various events (indeed, all events) that occur in your life in order to better control the feelings you generate. And necessarily, as you do this over and over again, such as over four to six weeks, your new way of responding to events in turn becomes habitual, just like the old way was before. This is the ideal situation, as you are now taking greater control over the new reality you are creating, which includes the new feelings that are necessarily a very large part of it.

So how can you change the way you think? We know all learning is a gradual, evolutionary, and repetitious process, and involves passing through four levels of incompetence/competence. The first level is unconscious incompetence, where you lack a particular skill or ability but don't know it. The second level is conscious incompetence, where you lack a particular skill but now you know it (i.e., someone has pointed this out to you). The third level is conscious competence, where you "know that you know" how to do a thing particularly well. The final level of learning is unconscious competence, where you do automatically or instinctively what you are able to do well and never have to think about it. At this point, your new behavior has become habitual—that is, fully ingrained—and is carried out totally at the subconscious level. (Note that the word *learn* has both the words *ear* and *earn* in it, which says a good deal about the process that is involved.)

Returning to the **A-B-C** process, we see that the thoughts in **B** (whether positive or negative, rational or irrational) act as the connecting link or bridge between the initial event (an occurrence in **A**) and the subsequent feelings in **C.** This sequence of events is one of natural cause and effect, and clearly shows the process we all follow when we engage in the activity we call thinking.

In this regard, it's key to note this important fact: Feelings themselves (**C**) do not represent the absolute truth about any given situation. They are simply a reflection of the particular thought or thoughts that preceded them (**B**). So if you want to overcome hurtful feelings (e.g., pain and suffering) in your life, you have only one recourse: Knowing you cannot change your feelings by trying to change your feelings, you must focus instead on the thought or string of thoughts you have adopted that caused those feelings in the first place. These things—*thoughts*—you can change!

In reality, a great many of your thoughts in response to a given event or happening have a large, self-absorbed egoic component to them—a huge dose of *me* ("Why is this happening to me??!! &%&!!?? Why me?")? This necessarily distorts your interpretation of the event and in turn the thoughts you adopt in response to that event. This is not unlike being overly paranoid about certain events or situations that happen in your life—believing that the world is out to make a mess of your life and you very miserable as a result. But what actually happens is the exact opposite: You make yourself very miserable by the process just described; at the same time, you make your life a mess as well.

Let me explain. We are all used to having positive, uplifting feelings that follow from a certain event or situation that we welcome. We readily accept such feelings as valid and realistic, as reflecting reality ("Wow! Things are really great."). But, of course, they do not. These feelings only represent how we have interpreted (i.e., evaluated and internalized) the initial activating event itself.

On other occasions, we react to an event we don't like with negative, depressing thoughts and feelings ("Ugh! Things are really awful."). Again, we fall into the trap of accepting these feelings as being valid and realistic, and hence reflecting reality. Of course, they do not. Therefore, to deal with feelings of all kinds, whether uplifting or depressing, welcomed or unwelcomed, a person has to go back and focus on the often twisted, distorted, and irrational thoughts that caused them in the first place.

Here's another example. Assume Molly didn't win the competition to become the new creative director at the advertising agency where she worked. This is **A.** This activates her personal belief system, and she concludes she is incompetent, unappreciated, and worthless. This is **B.** Consequently, she is upset, disappointed, and angry. This is **C.** Note that if her emotions are allowed to linger, unchallenged and unchanged, the odds are very small indeed that she will ever get promoted to such an important position.

The final part of the assessment process involves something called reframing. After assisting the client to identify the illogical, irrational, or faulty beliefs that are at play, the therapist works with that person to challenge the negative thoughts themselves, and to reassess and reinterpret the situation in a more positive and realistic light. The client benefits from a more accurate and rational personal belief system as well as healthier and more effective coping strategies.

From this example, the therapist would help Molly come to realize that not succeeding at a single competition is not a life-threatening event—that it is not conclusive evidence on its own that she is incompetent, unappreciated, or worthless. As well, Molly would be encouraged to use this as a learning experience to better prepare herself for future competitions. After all, she has at least 80 percent of her career still ahead of her.

For example, she could commit to improving her professional skills in general, or her interview and interpersonal skills in particular. In other words, she could inquire about the areas where she was found to be weaker than the other candidates, especially the one who was ultimately chosen, and begin immediately to take specific steps—whether a self-study program, a training course, or mentoring sessions—to improve on these.

Taking Responsibility for Your Thoughts

"Human beings, by changing the inner aspects of their minds, can change the outer aspects of their lives."

—William James (1842–1910),
American psychologist and philosopher;
author of *Principles of Psychology* (1890)

The need for each of us to accept personal responsibility for each and every aspect of our life (beginning with the quality of our thoughts) reminds me of this story about a construction worker. As he is opening his lunch pail to eat one day, he mumbles, "Peanut butter sandwiches. That's all I ever get are peanut butter sandwiches!" So his buddy says to him, "Why don't you ask your wife to make you something else?" And he replies, "I'm not married. I make my own lunch."

Isn't it the same with life? Each of us creates our own circumstances; we all "make our own lunch." (Read "create our own reality," no matter how twisted or irrational it may be.) Consider this: We have what we've got by doing what we've been doing, thinking the way we have become accustomed. It's simple enough. If what we want in the future is different from what we've got in the present, we have to change what we've been doing!

The following schematic on page 97 shows the challenge we all face in more detail.

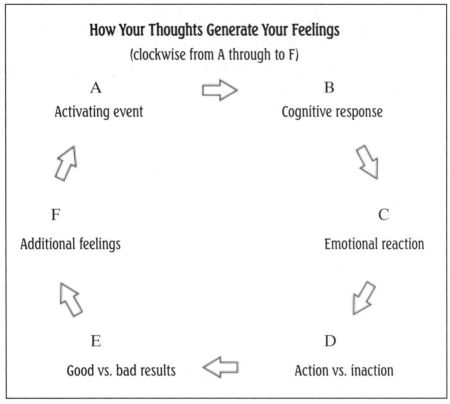

Figure 2

"There is nothing either good or bad but thinking makes it so."

—William Shakespeare (1564–1616),
English playwright and poet,
from *Hamlet* (1602)

Action vs. Inaction

To understand this chart, follow the sequence of events from **A** to **F** and carefully note what happens. (**A**, **B**, and **C** have already been discussed.) This is something that plays out several times a day in your life and invariably makes it either a very good day or a very bad one, or somewhere in between.

Some observations: First, inaction is a very real possibility if the cognitive and emotional response to **A** is negative (i.e., corrupted by faulty, illogical, or irrational thinking). I submit that this is not an acceptable outcome. Second, there are several entry points where intervention is possible to re-evaluate **B** (i.e., opportunities to interrupt the pattern and change the conclusion that has been reached). For example, it could occur after **B, C, D, E,** or even **F.** And third, if your additional feelings (**F**) are negative and totally discouraging (i.e., you expect to get only poor results no matter what you do), then this itself becomes another activating event (**A**), and the whole cycle repeats itself just like a closed loop. This is like being on a fast-moving train that is picking up speed; it's extremely difficult to get off.

Clearly action, which begins with rational, logical thinking, is the only outcome that takes you somewhere you want to be, versus inertia, which keeps you exactly where you are and don't want to be. It's one of the key concepts in moving ahead, and turning your life around quickly and permanently.

Interestingly, there is actually a disease associated with inaction. The word for it is *otiosity.* Otiosity is the state or condition of being "oti-ose," meaning: (1.) at leisure; idle; indolent; (2.) ineffective; futile; sterile; (3.) useless; superfluous. I'm sure it is a term you don't want applied to yourself.

How You See Yourself

This brings us to a description of self-image psychology, which in essence says:

You become in your life the person you see yourself to be in your mind.

So how does this work? You have developed a series of filters or perceptual frameworks, called paradigms, that you use to see and interpret all the things that are going on in your life. These paradigms are a function of your individual beliefs, values, assumptions, and opinions that you have acquired during your upbringing.

The master paradigm you have developed is called your self-image. It answers the question "How do I see myself in every conceivable aspect of my life?" You have specific pictures in your head that range from very negative to very positive that depict how you see yourself as a student, an athlete, an artist, a writer, a musician, a dancer, a lover, a negotiator, a public speaker, a parent, a teacher, a salesperson, a manager, a cook, a planner, and so on. There are literally thousands of these images of self that together constitute your self-image. This paradigm can be compared to a pair of invisible eyeglasses you wear every day. And it is you who has created your very own prescription—meaning your own sense of self.

This lens necessarily affects the way you see everything all around you, including yourself, your future, and what you think you can or cannot accomplish in your life. The breakthrough comes when you understand you can change the way the world looks to you—but first you must take the time to change the artificial lens through which you view it.

The simplest truths are often the most powerful; they need only be understood, accepted, and internalized. What is the simple truth, then, that this book proclaims to all those who are hurting, who are looking for a way to move beyond despair and despondency to hope and happiness?

It is this: It matters not where you were born, who your parents are, how much education you have, what language you speak, what skills you have developed, or what successes or failures you have had. Nor does it matter what major challenges or difficulties you may be currently facing in your life. It matters only who you *think* you are—for if you change who you think you are (which is a primary purpose of this book), you automatically change who you are!

Each day finds you at a certain place in your life. This has to do with many things, including your physical, mental, emotional and spiritual health; your relationships with family and friends; your professional career; and your personal finances. Usually, many of these aspects seem to be just fine while others are not. So you may simply want to fine-tune a few things. At other times, you may want to make more radical and wholesale changes, perhaps involving an important relationship or the career path you are on.

Whatever is on your agenda, the way you think is by far the most critical factor. This is why the activity called critical thinking is such an important skill to understand and apply—indeed to perfect! Without it, you are lost and left to the mercy of chance and circumstance, such as these situations: "Gosh, I sure was lucky when I made that decision!" or "Darn, I sure didn't guess right when I decided to do that!" As a further aid to help you critically assess the way you are thinking today about certain challenges you may be having in your life, I again refer you to the Mind T.R.A.P. Exercise on page 221.

The Great Wheel of Life

Consider how you organize your time and focus your energy on a daily basis. We have already described the key areas of life in general, those aspects that when added together determine the overall quality of life you enjoy.

The following depiction on page 101 helps conceptualize the fact that there are six key areas, and each is like a spoke in a large wheel. Note also that there is both a lower as well as an upper section, each with three components that interact and compound their effects. Again, the principle of cause and effect applies: **A** leads to **B** leads to **C,** and so forth. Note that Lady Luck, even with the best of intentions, can only do so much regarding the way your life is unfolding and the quality of life you are enjoying. This challenge is mostly left in your capable hands. (Hmmm. Would you rather it was in someone else's hands?)

You need to make it your business to feel content almost all of the time (say, 95 percent!). Otherwise, you will naturally drift off in the opposite direction and risk not realizing your full potential.

We know any wheel is only as strong as the central, supporting spokes that make it up. Hence if one or more of these is missing, the wheel becomes distorted in shape and invariably begins to wobble when put in motion. Like a car with a flat tire going down the road, you will hear a loud *whop! whop! whop!* that indicates something is seriously wrong. As well, if the distortion is significant enough, the wheel will totally collapse, as can happen with your life. Also note that your true Self—who you are—lies at the center or hub of this wheel and necessarily affects everything that lies within the circumference of the wheel.

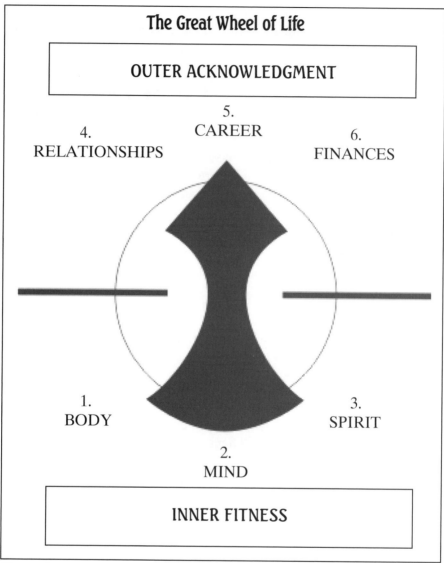

Figure 3

The wheel itself is rotating rapidly on a daily basis; events, happenings, and occurrences of all kinds are constantly taking place. And, as is the case for any rotating device, the activity is fastest on the outer perimeter (where you actually experience your life) and slowest at the very center.

This center, in fact, is not moving at all. Here, everything is peaceful, everything is still, everything is calm. So we see that your essence and the center of this wheel are exactly the same: You are peace, you are stillness, you are tranquility at your core. All are facets of pure love.

The three factors shown at the bottom of the circle are internal and relate to your person: (1.) your physical body; (2.) your mental faculties; and (3.) your spiritual Nature. These three constitute what I call your "inner fitness" factors. The next three shown at the top are external factors and relate to the world outside of your personal Self: (4.) your relationships (i.e., family and friends); (5.) your professional career; and (6.) your personal finances. These three constitute what I call your "outer acknowledgment" factors. In other words, the state or robustness of the last three factors is determined exclusively by the state or robustness of the first three. Each of these six areas can be measured in any number of ways, and the results can range from terrible to terrific.

Here's the point: When you are on solid footing, when your internal factors are all at or near the excellent level, this inevitably will be acknowledged or manifested in your everyday life—namely the three factors that are external to you. You likely will have healthy, meaningful relationships and be progressing well in your chosen career, and your finances will all be in order.

We know everyday events and happenings cannot and will not go perfectly all the time. Something called Murphy's Law—which says whatever can go wrong, will go wrong and just at the most inopportune time— invariably will show up at your doorstep as an unwelcome and uninvited guest. On these occasions, you will need something to carry you over the precipice, the great divide between dealing successfully with a major challenge or succumbing to it. In my own case, I had to succumb to challenges several times in my life (and endure the gut-wrenching pain that came with them) before I learned how to deal with them and move on.

The imperative, then, is to ensure you are making constant, measurable improvement in the first three key areas—namely in body, mind, and spirit which is the main focus of this book—thus leading to a proper balance among all six areas such that each is nurtured and gradually improved upon. In this way, a synergistic effect is created and incredible momentum generated. The ultimate goal is to have each area produce its own amount of joy and fulfillment, in turn making its own significant impact on the greater whole, thus creating a very meaningful, rewarding, and satisfying life.

Your Collective Consciousness

A problem we all have is how to better understand the quality or status of our thinking at any one point in time. So what can be done? Here is one suggestion. You can gain clear and unobstructed insight into your opinions, beliefs, and understandings about you and your world by closely monitoring what you say when you talk to yourself. This is that little voice inside you that never stops espousing on every subject under the sun.

An analogy is you can squeeze an orange, collect the juice that comes out, then taste it to determine if it is bitter or sweet. In other words, you can decide that bitter juice equals bad thoughts and sweet juice equals good thoughts. Now consider your own situation. When life puts the squeeze on you, which invariably it will do from time to time, how do you react? Do you send out negative or positive signals in direct proportion to the degree of the discomfort? Or do you take everything in stride and deal with it from a position of strength and inner knowing?

As you go about your everyday activities, you can pause, listen, and closely analyze what you are saying to yourself. It's often a two-way conversation that first takes one position on a given subject, and then another and another. It's not unlike listening to a heated debate between two people, each of whom passionately thinks he is right. This self-talk or internal verbalizations gives you an indication of the quality of your thinking on any topic you may be thinking about.

If you take the time to become aware of this inner dialogue and analyze it carefully, it will show you to what extent you are using one or more of the following: pre-judgments; total absolutes, over-generalizations, over-simplifications, gross distortions, simplistic rationalizations, or false assumptions in the way you are now seeing the state of affairs in your world. You can never hope to move beyond total helplessness when you choose to engage in erroneous, illogical, or irrational thinking. You are doomed to live a life of mediocrity at best.

> "Love all God's creation, both the whole and every grain of sand. Love every leaf, every ray of light. Love the animals, love the plants, love each separate thing. If you love each thing, you will perceive the mystery of God in all; and when once you perceive this, you will, from that time on, grow every day to a fuller understanding of it until you come at last to love the whole world with a love that will then be all-embracing and universal."
>
> —Fyodor Dostoyevsky (1821–1881),
> Russian novelist;
> author of *Crime and Punishment* (1866)

Seven Primary Enemies of Critical Thinking (Annex 6)

* **Pre-judgments.** A person goes about his daily activities with a long list of pre-judgments (aka prejudices) firmly embedded in his mind concerning almost every aspect of his life. Examples: opinions/beliefs about race, religion, culture, politics, poverty, wealth, crime, marriage, alcohol, illness, depression, work, sports, leisure, retirement, etc. The list is endless.

* **Total absolutes.** A person sees almost everything in her world as being either black or white, with no middle ground. Example: "Because my grades in high school were consistently low, I will never find a good job."

* **Over-generalizations.** A person believes that one situation or occurrence can be expanded to apply to all similar situations. Example: "No one in my family ever went to college, so there's clearly no hope for me either."

* **Over-simplifications.** A person sees a situation and comes to a quick conclusion without proper analysis of all the facts available. Example: "Because my writing skills are so poor, I can never hope to become an English teacher."

❋ **Gross distortions.** A person sees a situation in exaggerated ways, often due to emotional overtones. Example: "I'm not as attractive (pretty/handsome) as some other people I know, so I'll probably never get married and raise a nice family."

❋ **Simplistic rationalizations.** A person comes up with supposedly rational, plausible explanations or excuses to justify and support his beliefs and actions, often (but not always) without being aware that these are not the real motives.

❋ **False assumptions.** A person projects into the future and comes to a certain conclusion, often negative, based on past experiences. Example: "I've never excelled at anything important in my life up to now, so there's no way I will excel in a business career. It's obvious I don't have what it takes."

At its core, critical thinking is really an exercise in common sense. However, all too often, a person's focus is more on the conclusion he has already decided upon (often based on subconscious beliefs or emotional concerns and preoccupations) rather than the process she needs to follow in order to come to a more logical, rational, and well-thought-out conclusion.

The Power of Thought

"All that a man achieves and all that he fails to achieve is the direct result of his own thoughts. In a justly ordered universe, where loss of equipoise would mean total destruction, individual responsibility must be absolute. A man's weakness and strength, purity and impurity, are his own and not another man's; they are brought about by himself, and not by another; and they can only be altered by himself, never by another. His condition is also his own, and not another man's. His suffering and his happiness are evolved from within. As he thinks, so is he; as he continues to think so he remains."

—James Allen (1864–1912),
English writer and poet;
author of *As a Man Thinketh* (1902)

Knowing How to "Not Think"

"Meditation brings wisdom; lack of meditation leaves ignorance. Know well what leads you forward and what holds you back, and choose the path that leads to wisdom."

—Siddhartha Gautama (c. 563–483 BCE),
Indian prince and Spiritual Master,
and founder of Buddhism

A Quiet Mind = A New World

In Part 3, we look in more detail at how you can *not think* in the Now, in the "passive" mode of mind. In this regard, consider the following:

For most people, the inner journey is the journey of last resort; they go there only after they discover the outer journey doesn't work.

What a shame, for the inner journey is the only one that has any meaning, any substance, any real joy.

The inner journey referred to here is the place of no-thoughts, of no-mind, of stillness, or what is called the small space or gap that's known as unconditioned or "pure" consciousness. It occurs in Now, the seemingly fleeting yet ever-present present moment, that particular point in time when everything happens (the "active" mode of thinking) or doesn't happen (the "passive" mode). It's here where your inner consciousness and eternity intersect; in fact, it's the only place they intersect.

Pain and Suffering

It's in stillness where you come to know your Source, and, in turn, who and what you are. As such, the inner journey facilitates revelation through surrender to what is, which could be called "pure" understanding, meaning understanding that's not perverted or contaminated by the world of form, which includes often silly thoughts, silly ideas, silly assumptions, silly notions, and silly beliefs.

Not surprisingly, most people have experienced some pain and suffering at various times in their lives, and they necessarily carry this around with them every day. This is referred to as emotional scars or baggage. Everyone has this—emotional pain of one kind or another—and it lies buried deep in his psyche. But it's never too far from the surface, and it often represents a serious problem.

For one thing, such baggage is usually quite heavy; it holds you back from moving on and fully enjoying life. In other words, it weighs you down, saps your energy, and wears you out. We know everyone heals quite quickly from a broken leg but almost no one heals quickly from a broken heart or a diminished, even shattered, spirit. A physical injury simply heals itself while an emotional injury does not, even though many years may pass. It just sticks around, lies low, and continues to fester. Then, whenever the right occasion arises, it instantly pops back to life. If you suffer from insecurity, simmering anger, or deep regret, as many people do, this can usually be traced back to some prior event, to unhappy or traumatic experiences you went through as you grew up and experienced life.

Most people believe that pain and suffering are an integral part of life, that there is little or nothing they can do to avoid them. Yes, bad stuff will continue to happen in your life, and I'm sure you have noticed that. But you don't have to experience deep pain and suffering—which can burden and overwhelm you, or even render you totally helpless—as a result. Why? It's because we know an event of any kind comes with no particular emotions, either positive or negative, attached to it. It is totally neutral in its original form. It's how you interpret the event and internalize it that brings on any joy and elation, or pain and suffering.

Necessarily, whatever happens as your life unfolds, happens. In this sense, you have little or no choice. And you will either deal with it from a position of strength or a position of weakness. The former allows you to move on, whereas the latter holds you back. It can even drag you down to the depths of depression and despair, often to a point where the most you can hope for is to survive. Needless to say, life isn't very enjoyable, productive, or meaningful when all you are trying to do is survive.

If you have ever had one, you know a major depression is an extremely dark, desolate, and lonely place to be. The trauma is often so severe that it forces you to come face-to-face with your inner Self, your essence. For some, this represents a unique opportunity to explore this important aspect of their life, probably for the very first time. This can be the upside. But for others, there is only a downside. Many people who are suffering from deep depression are unable to do any serious introspection or reflection at all due to the painful and debilitating nature of their condition. (This was certainly the case for me.) They are totally overwhelmed by their present state, and have no idea how to deal with it or get out of it. It's likely the more pain and suffering you have had yourself, or witnessed among friends or loved ones, the more interest you will have in this subject—namely in healing, in wellness, in wonderment—in living a life of no more suffering.

Naturally, as your life unfolds, you are bound to have a certain number of unwanted events arrive at your street address, knock on your door, and, although not welcome, invite themselves right in. So here is my suggestion. Yes, you can hope for the best, but you should diligently and methodically prepare for the worst, as this is what may very well happen. This necessarily requires you to commit to doing some serious work, to acquiring some valuable skills, to embarking on an important journey. The information presented here is intended to start you down this path.

The goal? It is to inoculate yourself, so to speak, when you are feeling relatively well to the possibility of extreme pain and suffering in the future. This necessarily requires doing some serious self-study, reflection, and personal growth. More specifically, this means holistically improving your physical, mental, emotional, and spiritual health as much as possible. This way, you will develop an immunity of sorts to pain and suffering of virtually any kind, including trauma, much like a needle can inoculate you against the measles, diphtheria, and tuberculosis.

Research shows that you can rewire your brain to your advantage. This will lessen the possibility of ever experiencing a serious depression, or, should you have a relapse from a current situation, the odds are favorable it will be less intense and of shorter duration. It also shows you can rewire your brain to recover from traumatic brain injuries of various kinds. This ongoing research falls under the promising new science called neuro-plasticity. What follows expands upon the importance of no-mind as part of your various thinking options. Its purpose is to clearly distinguish between and highlight the importance of "passive" thinking versus "active" thinking. Indeed, the former, the "passive" or meditative state, represents an essential component in any comprehensive and lasting self-healing regimen.

Two States of Mind

Consider the two primary ways you can use your mind. The first is the "active" mode, where you simply let your thoughts (some welcomed, others not) create your reality. The second is the not-thinking or "passive" mode, where you defer to simple awareness to do this—an awareness that results automatically when you allow what is to be, no matter what it is and just as it is. We have already seen that these two states of mind are two very different worlds and create two very different experiences, and each plays a critical role in how you live your life.

It must be emphasized that the "active" mode of thinking is not the highest form or state of mind. Why? Consider these reasons:

1. Common, everyday thinking deals primarily with petty and transitory concerns and preoccupations, and seldom with discovering truth,

2. It occurs haphazardly and involuntarily, mainly in reaction to random stimuli in the external environment, and

3. The thinking mind is necessarily limited in scope and ability, as the information available to it is only a small fraction of all the wisdom and intelligence that's available in un-manifested form, in the vastness, yet simplicity, of "space" consciousness.

Conjecture versus Insight

Knowing there are only two very different states of mind, we can explore a conjecture versus an insight as each relates to truth. We regularly have thoughts that are based on conjecture about the unknown; it's in our nature to try to understand everything. And we often have thoughts that are based on insights about truth. As we engage in these activities, it should also be noted that most people have considerable difficulty understanding the difference between thoughts and insights, something that will now be addressed.

Hmmm. A conjecture about the unknown. Okay, now I'll use my mind (thoughts) to try to understand that. Hmmm. An insight about truth. Okay, now I'll use my mind (thoughts) to try to understand that. Either way, the result is always a thought or a series of thoughts, whether complicated or quite simple, and these thoughts necessarily are only a poor approximation of what they are attempting to describe.

Note that we soon replace any one conjecture with another conjecture, and yet another and another, whereas a truth—whether recognized as such or not—is timeless and eternal; it lasts forever; it never changes.

I suggest an insight in its original form is not a thought, at least not in the same sense that we have other thoughts. This is because it is a truth that presents itself to us in stillness, in no-mind. This way, we see that an insight is not a product of the mind; it is a product of no-mind. An in-sight is an asking, looking, seeing within; it's not an out-sight, a simplistic view or assessment of the physical world that exists all around us using any number of our five senses (all of which are limited and hence quite inaccurate), an activity we call perceiving or observing.

Who Am I?

So how does all this relate to you when you ask yourself the question "Who am I?" Interestingly, who you are and stillness are one and the same thing. Your true identity cannot be found in the avalanche of conscious thoughts that bombard your consciousness on a regular basis. Seldom if ever can great insight or wisdom come out of total chaos, what may also be called randomized anarchy. To realize your Self or true essence, you must spend time in stillness. To note, you experience individual instances of stillness all the time: a little slice here, a little slice there, just like the sun occasionally peeks through clouds on an overcast day.

From a personal perspective, these gaps occur between the individual thoughts your mind is having, or more correctly, between the thoughts you are allowing your mind to entertain. These gaps are very short intervals of time you spend while not thinking in no-mind. Other examples of gaps previously cited include the blank area around letters printed on a page, the pauses between words spoken in a conversation, and the silence between notes present in a musical score.

Consider this: While listening to a piece of music, how much meaning do you think comes from the music itself—the individual notes—and how much meaning do you think comes from the spaces—instances of silence—between the notes? Perhaps you could say in terms of sound or volume, the notes are most important; and perhaps you could say in terms of meaning and understanding, the intervals of silence between the notes are most important. (Or is it the other way around?)

Either way, there is absolutely no doubt about the following: The two must appear *together* to have maximum impact, to produce the maximum effect, to make the most sense. And so it is also with your mind. The two states of mind we have been talking about—mind and no-mind—must work together if you want optimum results.

Can you imagine what a musical composition would sound like if there were no gaps/pauses between the notes? A cacophony of confusion? A symphony of insanity? Note that these gaps—whether in a book, a speech, or a musical composition—in fact are silence. They are stillness, they are simplicity, and they are chock full of meaning. Who would have thought?

Awareness versus Understanding

Consider awareness or understanding for a moment as it relates to intelligence. There is a certain kind of intelligence (often measured as IQ in humans) regarding accumulated knowledge and mental prowess with which we are all familiar. But raw intelligence is not important regarding what we are discussing here, namely how to answer the question "Who and what am I?" It fact, it can be a very big hindrance.

If you look at a rock—a simple, everyday rock—it doesn't have any of this kind of intelligence at all but it does have a great deal of awareness or understanding concerning what it is. A rock accepts that it is a rock and doesn't indulge in a bunch of mind games about whether this is true or not. As a rock, it is at one with what it is, its self-identity. It just does what it is supposed to do: be (a rock).

The same applies to a tree, a flower, or a blade of grass. Each accepts what it is, and simply goes about being whatever it is. It lives in Now. It entertains no regrets about the past, or hopes or fears about the future. It is at one with what it is, its self-identity. It just goes about being what it is and doing what it is supposed to do.

Or consider a deer, a bird, a cat, a dog, a hummingbird, or a bumblebee. Each lives in the moment, accepting what it is and doing what it is supposed to do. It entertains no regrets about the past, or hopes or fears about the future. It is at one with what it is, its self-identity. It just preoccupies itself with being and doing.

As such, all these entities—each with a different level of awareness—live in a state of relative comfort (and likely with a certain amount of bliss) without temper tantrums, migraine headaches, panic attacks, bouts of depression, or acts of self-harm. Yes, you could argue that these entities are not really "thinking" entities at all, that they are simply born preprogrammed to be who they are and do what they are supposed to do; in other words, they act instinctively. And you would be correct.

So, some questions. First, why do we humans, who obviously have superior mental capabilities, have so much difficulty understanding and deciding who and what we are? And second, why, by our everyday deeds and actions, do we try to prove to ourselves and others all the time that we are right, that we are who we think we are, when at any point in time we don't know who we really are and are only guessing—fantasizing or philosophizing—about the whole thing? Good questions!

It's obvious we humans are more advanced in our mental capabilities, yet it seems this unique ability lies at the very root of our problem. The reality is that most people don't have any idea who they are or why they are here. So they just stumble about and struggle on, going through life in a state of total ignorance (note that in this case, ignorance is not bliss!), hoping that things will turn out for the best. Hmmm. A fruitless exercise in either hoping, or moping, or doping—all in a feeble attempt at just coping—for a lot of people.

Who Is Running Our Mind?

We humans use our natural intelligence to intellectualize and conceptualize, to assess/judge our past and ponder/imagine the future. This is normal and indeed can be helpful in many ways. For example, this way we can learn from our past mistakes and plan more carefully for the future.

The result is a series of thoughts our mind generates that usually arise in response to things—events, occurrences, or experiences—in our everyday life. These thoughts are often reactive and automatic, meaning they are unconscious and spontaneous, not unlike how non-thinking rocks, plants, and birds react that we have just talked about. In our case, however, we humans—unlike these other entities—seem to lack the natural, innate understanding about who and what we are, and so we automatically (and tragically) defer to the ego to make this decision for us. In other words, when in doubt, we default to the ego to find the answer.

So maybe, just maybe, we have to learn to better control our spontaneous mental reactions (note that spontaneous physical reactions cause nuclear explosions!) so that they don't lead us off in the wrong direction and mess us up, along with potentially doing harm to ourselves or others with whom we regularly interact.

We all know people who spend an inordinate amount of time each day worrying and complaining about various unimportant, irrelevant, and inconsequential aspects of their lives. It could be the weather, the morning traffic, their apartment, their car, their haircut, their dog, their bank account, their favorite sports team, their neighbors, their boss, their co-workers, or a close friend. All such thinking is unproductive and quite unnecessary, of course, and invariably contributes to their own sense of loss and despair.

But there is an even bigger problem that this scenario represents: Such people are attempting to understand reality—every facet of their life—through the cloak/veil of "active" thinking. In fact, most of us see ourselves through the cloak/veil of "active" thinking (whether it is productive or destructive) and thus answering, seldom correctly, some of the most important questions we face in life.

We've seen that we all have a very real choice regarding how we go about using our mind. At any time and for any reason, we can choose to experience the moment, be consumed by the moment, be immersed in the depths of Now—not all day but certainly for a good part of every day. In this instance, we are in the "passive" mode of mind. Here and only here, the channels of communication are wide open to a higher power, an intelligence or energy of unimaginable and indescribable proportions.

Alternatively, we can engage in "active" thinking where every aspect of our life is reduced to an ill-informed idea or conceptual abstract in our head. This includes our sense of self that becomes a thought-based, egoic creation that has no basis in reality. It's only a mental construct that is based on information we have randomly gathered from several obscure and often dubious sources, and it's all very suspect. Invariably, it is biased, incomplete, transient, and untested, and therefore false and totally misleading.

Living Fully and Meaningfully

So you yourself, in terms of your sense of self, have become a conceptualized, thought-based entity, a story that is part fiction and part fantasy, a poorly thought-out guess, a haphazard estimate, a concocted impression or poor approximation of who and what you are. You exist as a self-absorbed *me* based on your interpretation of your past, and a series of hopes and fears about the future. And because you're not sure you have all this figured out correctly, you automatically impose an always-striving-to-be-more requirement on top of this imaginary figure. Naturally you dread any notion that you are less than you think you are; that would make you wrong and that would burst your bubble. And Heaven forbid that this might happen!

But we know no one has ever encountered or been to the future, nor has anyone ever encountered or been in the past. (Yes, I know Michael J. Fox has been back to the future, but that doesn't count.) We do this only in our mind and necessarily we do it all in Now. Yet most people live each day as though the very next moment—whether thinking about the past or wondering about the future—is more important than the present moment or Now. But Now is all there is; and being ever-present, in Now, is where all truth lies, including the truth about you.

I suggest that "active" thinking without regular pauses for reflection is no way to proceed with the business of living fully and meaningfully with joy, passion, purpose, and compassion. It can only lead to more and more confusion, more and more frustration, and more and more suffering. As the Buddha has told us, a primary goal for each of us has to be no more suffering (or dissatisfaction, disappointment, despair, depression, or plain old unhappiness). Who would have thought that simple confusion about who and what we are could have such profound and negative consequences?

Being in the Now

To be in Presence is to be in stillness, and stillness is just another word for sacredness. To understand your own sacredness, you have to become still; you have to be present. If you are always consumed by thought, immersed in thought, lost in thought (note the word: *lost!*), then sacredness will always be unknown to you and you will never come to understand your true and only Self.

When you are truly present, when Presence is the base from which you operate your mind, you will begin to see that sacredness in fact is everywhere. It's not only inside you, it is literally all around you—in people, in places, and in things (including animals, birds, plants, trees, grass, the sky, the water, the air, the soil, etc.). It's easier to see this in certain places—the countryside, the beach, sacred shrines, various places of worship; there is much less noise and less density associated with these places. It's as though the structure or form of such places has a transparency or openness of some kind that allows their sacredness to shine through. It's not that other places—big cities, large crowds, or busy freeways—don't have sacredness inherent in them. They do. But such places are just so noisy, consumed, and overwhelmed with activity that this makes it more difficult to penetrate them and see what is inside.

It's the same with people. It's so much easier to see the sacredness in people who are open, peaceful, content, and at ease with themselves, who are at one with their true Nature. A newborn baby—whether sleeping, smiling, or screaming out loud—is a prime example of this innocence, of pure, authentic simplicity. Often it's noticeable in the elderly as well, those who have learned to tame, if not defy, their ego after so many years of living with it and, in the process, suffering from it. It's as if some older people are saying to themselves and others, "I don't want to *do* anymore, I just want to *un-do*," meaning they want to free themselves from the tyranny (i.e., the past conditioning) of their mind.

But even in places where sacredness is much easier to see and experience, some people are unable to unwind, refocus, and relax. They drink, they yell, they scream, they over-indulge; it's their way to escape from their pain, their frustration, their dis-ease, their dis-comfort, their dys-function. Such people are simply in overload. They are insensitive and over-stimulated to the point that they are blind to what many others can quite readily see. Such people have allowed thought-forms to create their reality. In their mind, they are still struggling, still trying to erase their current understanding of reality, and the pain and suffering that comes with that reality. This is a recipe for failure, a failure that begins by being unable to see beyond the world of thought, beyond the world of form.

How Words Fail Us

We know thoughts are things, and it's no easy task to stop them from coming your way. They always will, and usually at a faster and faster pace unless you take certain steps and initiate specific action to stop them or at least slow them down. It's like being in a shooting gallery and the bullets that are fired keep coming and coming, and—*yikes!*—they're all directed at you! The solution is to purposely interrupt the pattern, the relentless onslaught, what some people see as an ongoing nightmare or horror, and who desperately want to escape from that horror.

Coming to some conclusion about your essence doesn't begin with a flurry of thoughts. It begins with a realization, an appreciation, or an inner *knowing* that you then try to express in words because that's how the mind works. Necessarily, trying to describe a phenomenon as profound as who and what you are is an extremely difficult and challenging (in fact impossible) task for anyone. Have you noticed how hard it is for me to try to explain it to you here, in this material? How many others throughout history have had similar difficulties?

So it needs to be stated, clearly and unequivocally, that you will never be able to describe your essence in actual physical words, no matter what language you speak or how advanced your language skills may be. For whatever words you may come up with, they are only labels that represent mental constructs and artificial concepts. At best, they can be signposts or stepping-stones that point you in a particular direction. Truly, your essence is indescribable, incomprehensible, and unfathomable all at once. Forget about ever trying to describe it. You cannot. But thankfully, as we will soon see, you can *feel* it and in this way come to know it!

The "active" mind operates on the basis of structures and form—what could be described as unconscious living—and tries to understand everything it encounters on the basis of structures and form. But it cannot. As it continues to try, however, you often fail to note that things are already working out at each instant in time, this very second—in fact at any given moment—in Now. These are little pockets of pure perfection!

To prove this point, take a few moments and become present. Be one with Now. Start by closing your eyes...and notice what happens...as you slowly begin to shift your attention...to what is...at that particular point in time. In the moment at hand. Next, simply allow this what is—whatever it is—to be. *Just as it is.* No questions. No judgment. No interpretation. Simply surrender and accept, wonder and rejoice.

To better understand the experience, let's observe together what happens. As you gently shift your attention away from the constant flurry of thoughts and concerns that are always going on in your mind to focusing only on what is, you enter Presence and deep peace. Here, emptiness or no-thing-ness is your primary reality. Just bask in it; fully accept it; deeply experience it. As well, in the background, you will become aware of many sounds and sensations that are an integral part of this experience. These may include the wind as it blows, the trees as they bend, the waves as they ripple, the birds as they sing, the clock as it ticks, the cars as they pass, the child as he shouts, and the dog as it barks; you may also sense the sun as it shines, the trees as they tower, the flowers as they bloom, the grass as it grows, the earth as it supports all that gently rests upon it. When your mind is open, quiet, and receptive, a whole new world miraculously unfolds and presents itself to you in its most natural, uncomplicated, and unblemished state.

Here, in this place, you will find the peace, quiet, and serenity that have previously eluded you. In each moment, at any point in time, every "thing" is already as it should be. Every thing is in harmony, every thing is in sympathy, every thing is at peace with the Universe. In Presence, you won't find any of the litany of problems and worries that you otherwise believed existed, as they do so only as (worn-out) thoughts in the confines of your myopic mind. In stillness, in the place of the sacred, you have no problems for the sacred is beyond form, it is beyond confusion, it is beyond any doubt.

The Healing Process

Remarkable things happen when you spend time in Presence. You begin to see that many of the things that occurred to you in the past—often some extremely tragic things (a failed relationship, an unexpected job loss, or a serious health concern)—were all necessary to bring you to where you are today. Otherwise, if things had always been quite good or even so-called "perfect" in your life, you wouldn't have acquired the wisdom and knowledge you have today to move beyond the place where you once were.

If you think about it, two things may well apply. One, that temporary place wasn't that great anyway and two, something likely would have happened eventually that would have made that place untenable or intolerable. In this way, a cleansing, a healing, a sort of purification takes place and along with it a new contentment, a new appreciation of who and what you are, and why you're here.

Strange as it may seem, it often takes a great fall, a tragedy, or a calamitous event of one kind or another to wake you up to what is really important—*really* important—in your life. As a result, you acquire a whole new appreciation of life and an understanding of yourself from such an experience. Instead of seeing an occurrence like this only as tragic and hurtful, as you probably initially did, you come to see it as a blessing in disguise; you needed it to happen in order to push out an old reality and allow a new one in (however slowly) to take its place.

Consider this statement: *Fall far, rise even higher.* It articulates in a unique and succinct way a powerful spiritual law. It implies that a great fall in your life is often a precondition to having a significant increase in awareness, in understanding, in acceptance. In this regard, this comment by German-Swiss Jungian psychologist Marie-Louise von Franz (1915–1998) is noteworthy: "The only way the Self can manifest is through conflict." In fact, a fall represents a window of opportunity, indeed a blessing that forces you out of your comfort zone and old, tired, repetitive way of thinking. In turn, this allows you to live your life at a higher level of consciousness, with more understanding and acceptance, with more joy and meaning.

Take a moment and think back over your own life. Has not each fall helped you rise a little higher? Of course, some probably just knocked the wind out of you, whereas others may have brought you to your knees. But after you got back up, shook yourself off, and began to put the pieces back together again, you knew you were stronger and wiser for the experience. You now knew a little more about your Self—who and what you are. This is life changing! This is truly living.

Selflessness versus Selfishness

Anyone living in the unconscious state, consumed by the past and future, is constantly trying to complete his insufficient and limited sense of self. The "more" syndrome is a fixation of the ever-present ego. Its constant preoccupation is to direct you to always attempt to *do* more and *have* more in its desperate attempt to help you *be* more. It's an insidious compulsion, in fact a dysfunctional and debilitating disease.

The irony is that life actually works in reverse. If you have a clear and accurate understanding of who you are, this in turn will allow you to do more and have more as a natural progression or extension of your very essence, your Being. When this is the case, this concern—the need to do more and have more—no longer represents a precondition to living fully and in harmony with life.

There is a huge—indeed unlimited—amount of joy in simply Being. For one thing, if you just allow yourself to be, you are able to do or not do as well as have or not have without feeling guilty about being lazy, dysfunctional, unproductive, or unworthy. These are no longer relevant and necessary preconditions to knowing happiness or experiencing bliss.

In other words, if people already knew who and what they were, and why they are here, they could give up the obsession of always trying to do more and have more in order to feel more worthy, competent, and relevant. Hence they could direct all of their energy, natural talents, and innate abilities toward more meaningful and productive pursuits that benefit humanity as a whole and not just themselves.

As has been noted, most of the problems throughout the course of human history have been because of some people who wanted to feel important, and prove to themselves and others that they are a "somebody." This is still the case today, and it always will be as long as there are people who allow their ego to run their life and in the process, foist their insecurities, frustrations, and unsatisfied wants and desires onto other people.

Today, we have a critical situation. There are more than seven billion souls on the planet—all fearful, vulnerable, and confused—who are running around trying to find a happy ending to their story, their sense of self, their notion about who and what they are, by using their mechanical, cognitive, thinking mind. And there is absolutely no hope of success in this regard. For simply doing more and having more for the sake of doing and having can never lead to a more complete and accurate understanding of their true Nature. Simply put, this is a trivial pursuit—a meaningless preoccupation that can only end in tragedy and total failure.

The Relationship Between Feelings and Truth

We now come to this question: How can you know when a particular thought or insight you have—whether it's an idea, a belief, or a concept you have—represents truth? For example, it could be something that answers the question for you: "Who am I?"

We know if you simply *think* about it, you cannot come to any well-informed decision on the matter because by doing so, you are just using more thoughts to try to understand other thoughts, and this can only lead to ongoing confusion and needless frustration. For example, using your mind to try to understand your mind is very much like trying to hold your right hand in your right hand. Give it a try. Good luck!

However, consider this:

Do you think it is an accident that **truth** *feels* good, that **understanding** *feels* good, that **peace** *feels* good, that **love** *feels* good?

Do you think it is an accident that **joy** *feels* good, that **giving** *feels* good, that **forgiving** *feels* good, that **compassion** *feels* good?

And note that these feelings are not false or fleeting; they are real, they are pure, they are powerful, and they are permanent. The fact is, your feelings are able to tell you what is in harmony with your innate Nature and what is not. And your innate Nature, of course, is your essence, your true identity. It is who and what you are!

Hence, we see when you discover and know at a deep spiritual level what is true—namely who and what you are, you will cease to suffer; and when you do not, you will continue to suffer. *Suffering, then, is the gauge.* It is the barometer that tells you whether you are living by knowing or by guessing, whether in truth or in darkness.

So where might you end up on the suffering scale yourself after a few years of knowing and practicing the lessons being taught here? I can give you my own answer in this regard. On a scale that runs from zero to 10, with zero being no suffering at all and 10 being totally impacted by it, your suffering index should be less than 1 (i.e., about 95 percent). Why? Because, on certain occasions, *you will forget who you are* and have to remind yourself of the truth. This remembering process is called *anamnesis*, the recalling of spiritual truths that lie buried deep in your psyche. This will hold you in good stead until you forget again a few minutes later!

The late Jim Rohn (1930–2010), American author and motivational speaker, shares this observation with us: "If the idea of having to change ourselves makes us fearful and uncomfortable, we can remain as we are. We can choose rest over labor, entertainment over education, delusion over truth, doubt over certainty. These choices are all ours to make. But while we may curse the effect, we continue to nourish the cause."

Wanting to be "special"—uncommon, distinctive, exceptional—is an obsession, a constant neediness, for many people. It arises because people want to feel important, to know they matter, that they are recognized as being, in one way or another, unique or different or better. The irony in all this is clear: If people really knew who and what they were, they would see that they already *are* important; they already *do* matter; they already *are* unique, worthy, and of value by their very Nature. But failing to know this, they go about seeking recognition and acceptance in a variety of other ways, all of which in the end are unsuccessful, fleeting, and unfulfilling.

You have probably noticed that every day, to gain a sense of their individuality or self-importance, people often say to each other things like "Heck, you think you have problems. Well, sit down and let me tell you about mine!" (This will only take a few hours!) Yes, let me tell you *my* story, let me tell you about *my* situation, let me tell you about *my* problems, let me tell you about *my* mess." So whether it is pity or praise (either will do), they want it, and they want it all the time.

Your Book of Fiction

People who have traveled some distance down the road of life have come to realize that physical things are unable to satisfy spiritual yearnings. They have also discovered that always looking to the next moment, the next moment, and the next moment—and always completely ignoring the present one—cannot bring any relief. Relief is impossible in the physical world, the material world of continuous thoughts, things, and happenings, whether in the form of money, property, fancy titles, or noteworthy achievement. Like any addiction, whatever you have is never enough.

Adding to your story only adds to your story; it doesn't bring you any closer to truth. Your book of fiction (that describes who and what you *think* you are) only gets longer and longer, but it will never transform itself into truth (non-fiction), no matter how long it is or how hard you work at it.

Imagine trying to build your whole identity on a personal history of what you have done in the past, along with a good measure of what you plan and hope to accomplish in the future. Remember: Neither the past nor the future actually exists; each exists only as an idea, a thought in Now. So here is the relevant question: Why would you put yourself at so much risk, basing your actual sense of self on such fragile and precarious ground, on such temporary and in fact imaginary things? Yes—why, why, why indeed?

The solution we are seeking here lies in practical spirituality, and knowing what it can do for you. This has nothing to do with religion in general or any one religion in particular. Rather, it involves learning about common spiritual themes and principles that most of the world's major religions eagerly share, and how to apply them in your everyday life.

The goal is clear: It's to live a life of more hope, more compassion, and more joy, one that is full of meaning, purpose, and substance. The path to this end has been laid out for you. You need only begin, knowing it's the journey that involves the *individual moments* that make up each day—and not the destination itself—that really matters.

If we all knew and practiced who and what we are, imagine how this would change the world as we know it today.

The "D-R-A-G" Factor (Annex 7)

D = doubts

R = regrets

A = anger

G = guilt

"Life does not consist mainly, or even largely, of facts and happenings. It consists mainly of the storm of thoughts that is forever blowing through one's head."

—Mark Twain (1835–1910),
American humorist, satirist, lecturer, and writer;
author of *The Adventures of Tom Sawyer* (1876)

Emotional scars such as doubts, regrets, anger, and guilt make people dysfunctional, fearful, and limited in their ability to live up to their full potential. They cause people to hide out in their comfort zone and avoid risk at any cost. For example, once hurt, people don't want to be hurt again. They hold people back; they literally act as a D-R-A-G on their development and well-being.

It's no surprise that most people have any number of emotional scars that they acquired at various times during their upbringing. After all, no one goes through life without several challenges and setbacks, successes and failures. These are simply the things that show up as we live, learn, and grow. Just as there are cuts, bruises, and scars that impact our physical bodies, there are also cuts, bruises, and scars that impact our mind, our psyche.

Compared to a physical scar, however, an emotional scar represents a particular challenge: It doesn't automatically heal itself. Because we invariably move on after any given emotional challenge, we think we are home-free, so to speak; we think we have put it behind us. But in many cases, we have not. The emotional scar lives on until we return to it and deal with it in some meaningful and constructive way. In the meantime, the scar, still alive and well, negatively impacts our mind by lowering our ambition, stifling our creativity, and draining our energy. This is not a recipe for living fully, joyfully, and in harmony with our true Nature.

Reflection and introspection as a result of daily meditation are valuable tools in this regard. Spending time in stillness helps bring about healing and understanding, peace and acceptance, in your own life. For example, consider the following scenario.

Assume for a moment you were born and raised without a past, and therefore had no hurtful memories lurking in your mind at all. In other words, whatever your current age or present situation, just assume you have no personal history or drawn-out story that defines you. Now, with this understanding firmly in place, how would you answer the following questions?

1. What 10 key qualities or character traits would you strive to develop, knowing they would bring love, peace, hope, and happiness in greater abundance into your life?

2. What would you choose to believe about your Self—namely who you are, what you're made of, and what you could accomplish in your life?

3. What incredible intention, amazing purpose, or phenomenal result would you pursue if you knew you could not fail?

EXPLANATION: Yes, you will fail if you don't even try; there is no doubt about that. But you will make some progress—likely only marginal at first but perhaps monumental later on—if you do. So *try*, because you owe it to yourself and others to make a difference. You want to manifest the magnificence that you are. The Universe is looking for a return on its considerable investment—in you (!), specifically in your body, mind, and spirit. You didn't expect that this wondrous and magnificent trip would be a free ride, did you?

"Here is the simple secret to happiness. Whatever you are doing, don't let past move your mind; don't let future disturb you. Because the past is no more and the future is not yet. To live in the memories, to live in the imagination, is to live in the non-existential. And when you are living in the non-existential, you are missing that which is existential. Naturally, you will be miserable because you will miss your whole life."

—Chandra Mohan Jain (1931–1990),
Indian mystic and Spiritual Teacher

Where Is Your Consciousness Focused? (Annex 8)

Go into stillness and immerse yourself in the "is-ness" of Now. What you will find there is wonderful, indeed incredibly vibrant and immensely profound. You will find your Self.

Most of us have never thought to ask ourselves "Where is my mind focused on a minute-to-minute and day-to-day basis?" and hence have no idea what our answer might be.

The question being asked here is: When you are alone, quiet and still, where does your mind go when it is free to wander? To find out, lie down on your bed or sofa and close your eyes. As you begin to relax, become aware of what your mind is doing and what thoughts are taking place without any effort on your part. Proceed to consider your first thought, and determine if this thought is about something from the past, the present, or the future. Repeat the exercise as each new thought enters your consciousness—the second, the third, the fourth, etc.—and determine what the subject of each one is.

When I first did this some years ago, I was quite surprised as well as disappointed, even dismayed. I found, if left to their own devices, my thoughts were focused on the *past* about 65 percent of the time (i.e., remembering and regretting that this or that had happened), on the *future* about 30 percent of the time (i.e., wondering what my life situation—my health, my relationships, my career, my finances, etc.—would be like three to five years from now), and on the *present* only about 5 percent of the time that prompted these questions: Where was I—at that very instant? What was I doing—at that very instant? What was I thinking, experiencing, and feeling—at that very instant?

Incredible! Past-future regrets, ruminations, hopes, and fears were dominating my consciousness. By doing this, I was reliving the past or pondering the future 95 percent of the time, leaving very little time—my most precious asset—to experience, enjoy, and learn from the present moment. A most unfortunate and wasteful way to go through life, it must be said!

In this regard, some have speculated that by age 65 or so (sometimes much earlier), many people simply relive/regret their past and worry/fret about the future pretty much all the time, meaning their life comes to an end (figuratively if not factually) far before it needs to.

Some Gentle Reminders (Annex 9)

Think, and there are some places you can go.
Not-think, and there is no place you can't go.

1. Regarding everyday events and happenings, you will *respond* to them if it is from Presence (with Presence simply being consciousness without thought), whereas you will *react* to them if it is from ego. There is a great deal of difference between the two. The former is from a position of strength/control and the latter is from a position of weakness/no control.

2. After a while, you will find you don't really need a formal method to meditate in order to enter Presence. Once you are doing regular, formal meditation, you will soon do this unconsciously as you go about your day (i.e., watch a child play, smell the aroma of freshly perked coffee, marvel at a flower, keenly observe a bird, watch the splendor of a sunrise/sunset, or routinely look in wonder at the pattern and shape of clouds in the sky).

3. One way to look at us humans is to see ourselves as comic characters (who generally lack a sense of humor) who are out of alignment with our cosmic Source.

4. The best music is a skillful combination of form (namely notes) and the form-less (namely the space between the notes). Each needs the other to fully express what they represent together, their One-ness, their aliveness. It's the same with life.

5. The conditions of your life are not here to make you happy; they are here to wake you up! Every obstacle/challenge is an opportunity to learn and grow—a door to realizing your Self, which is just another name for sacredness.

6. Believing you are a somebody or believing you are a nobody is simply ego; I suggest it is best not to give yourself—who you are—a name or label. In other words, just accept that you are indescribable (that sounds pretty good), really just a *no-thing* (oops!).

7. The thinking mind cannot recognize formless intelligence, meaning profound insights and simple truths. In other words, there are some *knowings* that to the thinking mind appear as not-knowing. (Geez! No wonder we're all so confused.)

8. Most people believe that if they think more, they will make better decisions. Wrong! The fact is, if you think *less*—by spending more time in no-mind—you will make better decisions. In the latter case, you have less ego and other petty distractions complicating the process and directing you down meaningless and unproductive paths.

9. Don't try to find enlightenment as a goal unto itself. Just disassociate yourself from your mind on a regular basis by going into silence. (This can involve both formal and informal meditation.) In the process, you will find enlightenment.

10. Many amazing things will happen to you in your life as you reach a higher level of consciousness. First, you will realize that there is no separation between you and every other thing on the planet. Second and more importantly, you will realize that there is no separation between you and your Source. Every thing in fact is "one" thing.

"When we find ourselves looking at the world and saying, 'There's nothing out there for me,' we should probably also look into our hearts and ask, 'If there's nothing out there, is there anything in here?' We need to examine our inner dialogue to discover where we might be blocking the conscious energy flow, then remove the ego, step out of the way, and let the fire of the soul shine through us."

—Deepak Chopra, MD (b. 1947),
Indian-born author of *The Spontaneous Fulfillment of Desire: Harnessing the Infinite Power of Coincidence* (2009)

"A quiet mind is all you need. All else will happen rightly, once your mind is quiet. As the sun on rising makes the world active, so does self-awareness affect changes in the mind. In the light of calm and steady self-awareness, inner energies wake up and work miracles without any effort on your part."

—Nisargadatta Maharaj (1897–1981),
Indian Spiritual Teacher and philosopher;
author of *I Am That* (1973)

"The mind, in proportion as it is cut off from free communication with nature, with revelation, with God, with itself, loses its life, just as the body droops when debarred from the air and the cheering light from heaven."

—Dr. William Ellery Channing (1780–1842),
American Unitarian preacher and philanthropist

"Silence demands space, space in the whole structure of consciousness. There is no space in the structure of one's consciousness as it is, because it is crowded with fears—crowded, chattering, chattering. When there is silence, there is immense, timeless space; then only is there a possibility of coming upon that which is the eternal, sacred."

—Jiddu Krishnamurti (1895–1986),
Indian philosopher, speaker, and social critic;
author of *You Are the World* (1972)

Knowing the Benefits of No-Mind

P
A
R
T

4

"Perhaps 'spiritual' means simply experiencing wholeness and interconnectedness directly, a seeing that individuality and totality are interwoven, that nothing is separate or extraneous, and that everything is spiritual in the deepest sense, as long as we are there for it."

—Jon Kabat-Zinn, PhD,
American author of
Wherever You Go, There You Are: Mindfulness Meditation in Everyday Life (1994)

Finding a Sanctuary: The S-A-D Factor (Stress, Anxiety, and Depression)

A major problem in society today is the increasing level of stress, anxiety, and depression that is impacting every aspect of life, and the difficulty the average person has in dealing with it. In fact, anxiety is recognized today as the number-one health concern in the world, as reported by both respected international organizations such as the World Health Organization (WHO) as well as individual countries themselves. Experts estimate that up to one-third of the general population is affected—either short-, medium-, or long-term—by significant mental or emotional challenges of one kind or another during their lifetime.

We see that a large number of people are stressed out on a regular, repeat basis. This is causing havoc in both family settings and places of work, as well as placing huge demands on national and local healthcare workers (including psychologists, psychotherapists, psychiatrists, pharmacists, counselors, social workers, etc.) who have to deal with the situation. The cost to governments and companies in lost productivity alone amounts to tens of billions of dollars each year—this at a time when many skilled workers and experienced managers of all kinds are in short supply due to the retirement of many who are part of the Baby Boom generation. The oldest in this group, born between 1946 and 1964, are now well into their late 60s.

Regarding the workplace and the incidence of depression, anxiety, and use of alcohol by workers, a study reported in the May 2009 issue of the *Journal of Occupational and Environmental Medicine* has come up with some interesting findings. Dr. Marjo Sinokki and her colleagues at the Finnish Institute of Occupational Health followed 3,347 employees aged between 30 and 64 for a period of three years. The goal was to rate the atmosphere in the workplace environment according to four primary descriptions: (1) encouraging and supportive of new ideas; (2) prejudiced and conservative; (3) nice and easy; or (4) quarrelsome and disagreeable.

In addition, employees were asked to note their feelings about team spirit, communications, the amount of pressure they were under, and how much control they had over their jobs. They were also asked about their social lives, where they lived, and what kind of healthcare services they could access. Their levels of depression, anxiety, and use of alcohol were then compared to their taking prescription antidepressant drugs.

The findings include the following: Those workers who felt team spirit in the workplace was poor were 61 percent more likely to have a depressive disorder. This group was also 55 percent more likely to be taking antidepressant drugs. No direct link was found with alcohol abuse or anxiety. The authors summed up their study by saying, "A poor team climate at work is associated with depressive disorders and subsequent antidepressant use."

Stress Is Everywhere

Stressful elements of various kinds are everywhere, and they include both internal and external stressors. Internal stressors are the result of negative emotional experiences you may have gone through as a child or young adult, and have left either temporary, semi-permanent, or permanent psychological scars. As a result, you may lack self-confidence; suffer from eating disorders, social anxiety, panic attacks, or insomnia; or have difficulty developing and maintaining close and loving relationships.

External stressors originate in the environment and are almost impossible to avoid. The information explosion is a prime example. Today, you are being impacted by as much information in a few weeks as those in previous generations were in a full year. Through mass advertising and aggressive marketing, you are being told what to eat, what to wear, what car to drive, what electronic gadgets to play with, what movies to see, what songs to listen to, how to be attractive, how to be fit and healthy, and how to spend your leisure time—in short, how to live almost every aspect of your life. As well, large pharmaceutical firms are constantly telling you to simply pop a pill to cure whatever ails you, implying you don't need to take any responsibility for your own behavior.

Another stressful area is the common work environment and the ever-increasing demands being placed on employees at all levels, people who are already struggling to juggle a variety of personal and family-related responsibilities. Globalization, and the rapid rate of change and increased competition that it represents, is only compounding the problem. Every country now competes with every other one, looking to survive, perform well, or even dominate the economic and geo-political landscape.

In this regard, we know all stressors you encounter are in fact benign (i.e., neutral) in their original form. It is only when you assign a certain meaning to them (say, on a scale from minus 10 through to plus 10) that they result in an emotional response of some kind. (To note, reactions to positive events can be as traumatic as negative ones, including getting married, the birth of a child, a new job, etc.) Here, your personal belief system plays a key role, as seen in Part 2. In other words, it's not the stressors themselves that cause problems; it's how you *interpret* them (i.e., your cognitive response to them), and this varies a great deal with each individual.

The mind and body are closely interconnected, and each affects the other. Working together, they detect and deal with stressors of all kinds as a defense mechanism, primarily to ensure your overall heath and physical survival. For example, when the mind encounters a stressor that says danger is present, the body experiences an *arousal response* of a certain magnitude as a warning. In this instance, you will experience an adrenaline surge, enhanced sensual acuity, and a rapidly increased heartbeat. However, if such encounters occur too often, are of a major proportion (such as repeated traumatic experiences in a war zone), and are fully accepted and internalized, your health can be seriously affected in a variety of ways.

For example, your immune system can be negatively impacted, making you more susceptible to a variety of diseases; you can develop debilitating symptoms associated with PTSD including extreme anxiety, fatigue, insomnia, and depression; and finally, you may develop chronic medical conditions such as cardiovascular disease and muscle-tension headaches. People who suffer from excess stress are also more likely to turn to alcohol or drugs in an attempt to self-medicate and escape (albeit only temporarily) from their predicament.

Things You Can Do

Thankfully most people are not in a war zone, although at certain times in their life they may think they are. If you have ever been extremely stressed or depressed, you know that it drains you of your energy, hope, and desire, thus making it even more difficult to do the very things you need to do to begin feeling better. Though there isn't a simple formula or quick fix to overcome depression, it is possible to make regular and meaningful progress. The key is to realize you do have an element of control. In other words, it is important to establish a baseline of activity. You begin this by doing several small things on a regular, daily basis. Once in place, you slowly increase these activities and explore slightly more challenging ones.

Here are some options available to you:

1. **Eliminate as many stressors as possible.** Organize your finances carefully to avoid going into debt; this involves setting up and following a detailed monthly budget comparing income and expenses. Don't go on a shopping spree as a way to feel better. Always take a day or two to think twice before committing to any major purchase. Organize the routine you follow at home and at work a little differently. Watch less (local, national, and world) news and grisly crime programs on TV. Take a college or university course in a subject that interests you. Consider a change in career. Set aside a certain amount of time each day for yourself. Learn to say no to those who make frequent and unnecessary demands on your time; this may include your partner/spouse, children, friends, and relatives. Develop and regularly practice better interpersonal skills such as mindful listening, empathizing, and clear, concise communications to avoid needless misunderstandings and unnecessary arguments.

2. **Find better ways to deal with the stress you cannot avoid**. Take time to relax and get sufficient sleep. Get organized by always having a definitive to-do list for important things to finish in

the next five, 10, 30, and 60 days. Set aside more time for yourself including indulging in an occasional sauna/hot bath or arranging for a weekly massage. Spend more time with family and friends whose company you enjoy and appreciate. Begin an exercise program, even something as basic as walking for 30 to 45 minutes a day. Spend more time outdoors at some activity that gives you pleasure and changes your mind, such as a visit to a beach, a bicycle ride, or a weekend trip to the countryside. Become an expert concerning the many ideas and approaches described in this book, especially critical thinking and mindfulness meditation, and practice them on a daily basis.

3. **Seek out community assistance.** Don't fall into the trap of thinking you have to do everything yourself. Increasingly, there are myriad offerings from community organizations, colleges, universities, and volunteer and mental health groups and associations in your local area to help you deal with stress and depression. Many have toll-free numbers and helpful Websites with advice on this subject. Consult your doctor and ask for a list of organizations to contact. Visit your local library or bookstore for books, CDs, research studies, and articles on this subject. Check out video presentations and panel discussions by acknowledged experts on the Internet, including YouTube. Consider employing the services of a personal wellness or exercise coach. Sometimes a few simple ideas will get you started, but you must understand it is up to you to take the initiative.

4. **Finally, practice regular, daily mindfulness meditation,** which is a main focus of this book. There is more and more evidence each year that supports the benefits of this activity. Mindfulness uses your inner resources for healing and is easy to learn. (It does require, however, a certain amount of patience, openness, curiosity, and self-discipline.) As a natural way to deal with troublesome thoughts and emotions, it

is unique. It's available to you at any time, any place, and for whatever period of time you make available. And you don't have to pay to do it by the hour. It's free at a time when most things of any value are not. On this topic, I'm reminded of Abraham Joshua Heschel (1907–1972), Rabbi and theologian, who said, "Knowledge is fostered by curiosity; wisdom is fostered by awe." So meditate, and add some wisdom and awe to your arsenal of self-healing tools.

A Definition

Mindfulness meditation (also known as insight meditation) is a mental activity wherein you remember to pay attention in the moment. This means a combination of three things: (1.) being present-centered, namely directing your full attention to the present moment; (2.) being sensation-focused, such as on your regular breathing; and (3.) being process-absorbed, which involves sustained attention on the process that is chosen rather than on individual occurrences within that process.

Mindfulness meditation is not a ritual, dogma, or even a methodology. It's a practice that takes you into stillness that in turn leads to an enhanced sense of awareness. In this practice, you learn to attend to the mind rather than follow it; you engage the mind instead of being engaged by it. The ultimate purpose of the initiatory life is to become one with your essence, to deeply reside in Being, and allow that depth of existence to impact and inspire your whole life.

The Initiatory Life and Transcendence

When you embark on the path of mindfulness meditation, you are living the initiatory life, one that involves taking proactive steps toward better understanding life's many mysteries. Life's biggest mystery, some would say, is who and what you are, your essence, your innate, inborn Nature that is unimaginable, indescribable, and ungraspable. In a real sense, then, through mindfulness meditation, you are moving toward a better understanding of your true identity at the deepest level.

Exercises in mindfulness are exercises in transcendence and involve moving beyond or transcending the ongoing chaos, turmoil, and insanity of the everyday world to a new and higher level of consciousness. The goal is always the same: an end to suffering. Note that transcendence is not something that is in another place or at another time, and you have to go out and earnestly try to find it. It's where you are right now. It is easily within your reach and desperately wants to be embraced. It represents an energy or intelligence that's beyond your ability to fully understand, yet it is readily accessible when you spend time in stillness and experience the beauty, simplicity, and richness that can be found there.

Transcendence is not an impractical, abstract concept. It is a very direct and real experience, a liberating force that is accessible through various structured physical and mental exercises. This experience is characterized both by its effects (i.e., how certain parts of the brain are activated) as well as by its revelatory nature, meaning what you learn or come to understand from it.

People seek out transcendence for any number of reasons, often for a calmer, more meaningful/purposeful life and a more focused/perceptive mind. Although there is nothing more natural than your true Nature, we tend to function as humans in a way that focuses most of our energies on physiological, security, social, and self-esteem needs and wants. By doing this, we are always getting in the way of being able to experience transcendence as a liberating force and discovering who we really are. Thankfully, this tendency is beginning to change as the current surge in interest in spirituality around the world clearly shows.

When you function at this, the deepest level, you are no longer preoccupied with ego-centered concerns that include physical survival, personal competence, or social acceptance (i.e., "Gee, I hope everybody likes me!"). You will know peace, love, and joy unconditionally and naturally. Transcendence leads to enlightenment, and with enlightenment come understanding and uncommon happiness in all aspects of your life.

Transcendentalism has evolved as a respected philosophy that places an emphasis on the importance of the spiritual inner Self over the materialistic outer world. The teachings of Immanuel Kant, Georg Wilhelm

Friedrich Hegel, and Johann Gottlieb Fichte are prime examples. In its most simple terms, it could be said that this involves a search for reality and truth through wakeful awareness, an approach popularized in the mid-19th century by New England–based authors Ralph Waldo Emerson, Henry David Thoreau, and Walt Whitman in their numerous musings, writings, and lectures. Thoreau's comment "The question is not what you look at, but what you see" is particularly poignant regarding our discussion here.

Mindfulness is something you can participate in at any time or place in your wakeful state, not just during formal practice sessions once or twice a day. You could also incorporate it into simple, everyday activities including eating, walking, bathing, listening, watching, tasting, touching, smelling—any number of informal undertakings such as these. This way, you experience life and its everyday happenings at a deeper level, which allows you to relate and respond to them at a higher level.

Regarding eating, a study in the *Journal of the American Dietetic Association* (July 2008) shows that mindful eating can help you eat less and enjoy your meals more. The process involves eating slowly, chewing the food well, and putting your knife and fork down between each bite. As you eat, avoid any multitasking such as watching TV, reading the newspaper, texting, or talking on the phone. This allows you to direct your full attention to the task at hand. Consider this approach, along with keeping a detailed daily food journal, as part of your weight-management program.

Breathing

Breathing as a natural activity lies at the very center of mindfulness meditation. Breathing is a necessary and important bodily function that exchanges carbon dioxide for oxygen to ensure your physical survival, but it can also serve a much broader purpose. Through it, you can experience yourself as a living, fully functioning human being—opening then closing, presenting then surrendering yourself to the Universe. In mindfulness meditation, you use your breathing as a tool to come to know your true Nature, to discover and appreciate your real Self.

There are good reasons why breathing can play this role. Breath is life. It is what connects all the events in your life from birth to death. Breathing is something you always do, and it always takes place in the present; hence identifying with it allows separation between the present moment and past-future preoccupations. It is constant, predictable, and life-giving; as well, it is easily observable as an object of your attention. Breathing is not an active seeking-out activity that requires a lot of effort or intense concentration; rather it is passive and involuntary, an act of surrendering. In this sense, focusing on your breathing allows you to disengage from the "active" mode of thinking and engage with the "passive" mode of not thinking.

How to Meditate: Seven Simple Steps

You can teach yourself how to meditate by following these simple steps:

1. Find a quiet place where you will not be disturbed.

2. Sit upright in a comfortable chair with both feet firmly on the floor.

3. Set your timer for 15, 20, or 30 minutes, depending on the time you choose to make available.

4. Close your eyes (not mandatory, but it can help reduce visual distraction) and become an innocent, detached observer of "what is going on" in your mind.

5. Take deep, controlled in-breaths and deep, controlled out-breaths, with a deliberate, significant pause after each one.

6. Pick a simple word such as "blessings," a phrase such as "thank you" or "only love matters," or an image or symbol that is particularly comforting and soothing to you.

7. Repeat the word or phrase (or visualize the image/symbol) you have chosen over and over again with each out-breath. The monotony of the repetition will help calm you down and assist you in entering a state of deep peace and solitude.

Practice deep, controlled breathing for this exercise. First, observe your in-breath from start to finish. Be aware of the air entering your nostrils, traveling along your airway, filling your lungs, and finally inflating your chest and abdomen. Pause. Now, focus on the out-breath. Be aware of the air leaving your lungs, moving back up the airway, traveling out your nostrils, all the while deflating your chest and abdomen. Pause. In time, breathing this way while meditating will become automatic.

Mindfulness meditation creates a *relaxation response* throughout your body, the exact opposite of the arousal response that was discussed earlier. During mindfulness, observe your thoughts without either suppressing them or judging them. Act like an innocent, detached observer of what is impacting and engaging your mind. For each thought that presents itself, simply observe its contents and how it makes you feel; that's all. Then let it go.

The result? Over time, you will become more aware of how you react to any given stressor, have greater insight regarding the range of stressors your mind is currently dealing with, and have developed a better way of responding to such stressors in general and accepting them as a normal part of life. Stressors by themselves need not be troubling or debilitating; they just need to be better managed and controlled.

Suggested Exercises

Here is a meditation exercise for your consideration.

Choose a quiet setting where you won't be disturbed. While sitting with your back straight in a chair or against the wall on the floor, close your eyes and begin to shift your attention, ever so slowly, to your breathing. As you do this, take a few deep breaths and be aware of the sensation this creates in your nostrils and nasal passage; your chest and abdominal muscles; your shoulders and lower/upper back; your arms, wrists, and hands; your thighs, knees, and feet; as well as your neck, face, and skull.

Maintain your focus on your breathing; no thoughts, no thoughts. Just breathe in slowly, hold that breath, then breathe out slowly. As you continue to do this, inhale slowly, imagine this as God (or divine energy, universal consciousness, or whatever term you are most comfortable with) sending its love and joy into your mind/body. Now hold it; hold it; imagine this phase as God hugging, caressing, and comforting you; now begin to exhale slowly, and imagine this as you sending God's love and his blessings back out to every thing and every one in the Universe. Repeat this activity (gently bring in his love, hold it, hold it, feel its warmth and comfort, then slowly send it back out to the Universe) for 20 or 30 minutes.

A key aspect of meditation is repetition, the constant refocusing on your breath each time the mind wanders off, which invariably it will. It is the same as (bicycle) spinning, weight-lifting, or doing sit-ups to build muscle and increase endurance. Calming the mind is much like trying to catch a piglet at a county fair or holding a slippery, flapping fish in your hands. It's a challenge! Personally, I liken it to a series of punches (thoughts) hitting a punching bag (my mind), and I just notice this, accept it, and simply return to my natural size and shape (stillness). To note: It's more beneficial to meditate several times a day, however briefly, than extend the duration of a single escape.

Clinical Application of Mindfulness

Mindfulness is a particular form of awareness that has its roots in the Buddhist tradition that originated in India about 2,500 years ago and later spread to other neighboring countries in Asia. Dr. Jon Kabat-Zinn, working with his colleagues at the University of Massachusetts Medical School, first introduced mindfulness as a form of meditative practice to a modern medical setting in 1979. He founded a stress-reduction program, today known as mindfully based stress reduction, or MBSR, and applied mindfulness meditative practices to bring relief from stress, pain, and chronic illnesses.

The results were quite spectacular. News of his approach soon became widely known through his three books (see the Bibliography), research papers, articles in medical journals, and the many lectures and talks he has given. Patients positively impacted included those with chronic diseases, debilitating conditions, and psychological challenges including anxiety and panic. Dr. Kabat-Zinn has gone on to train hundreds of practitioners from around the world to carry on his important, groundbreaking work.

Meditation Retreats

A *Time* magazine dated August 4, 2003, features actress Heather Graham on its cover practicing transcendental meditation. The accompanying article by writer Joel Stein notes the virtual explosion in the number of people in America and elsewhere—most just normal people with jobs and families—who are taking up meditation as a daily exercise, typically 20 minutes twice a day. It highlights the London Buddhist Center, England; Shambhalla Mountain Center, Red Feather Lakes, Colorado; Maharishi University, Fairfield, Iowa; Seoul International Zen Center, South Korea; Insight Meditation Society, Barre, Massachusetts; Spirit Rock Center, Woodacre, California; Marpa Gompa Meditation Society, Calgary, Canada; and several Catskills hotels and centers in upper New York state as examples of the increasing popularity of this activity, saying that in the New York instance, the Borscht Belt is now better known as the Buddhist Belt.

Stein points out in his article that some meditators are also celebrities, listing regular practitioners such as Goldie Hawn, Shania Twain, Richard Gere, Al Gore, as well as Heather Graham. Graham starred in the TV series Twin Peaks in the early 1990s as well as several movies, including *Austin Powers: The Spy Who Shagged Me* in 1999. In 2001, she was voted by *People* magazine as one of the 50 Most Beautiful People in the World.

Stein goes on: "Meditation is being recommended by more and more physicians as a way to prevent, slow, or at least control the pain of chronic diseases like heart conditions, AIDS, cancer, and infertility. It is also being used to restore balance in the face of such psychiatric disturbances as depression, hyperactivity, and attention-deficit disorder (ADD)." He then cites Daniel Goleman, author of *Destructive Emotions* (2003), as saying, "For 30 years, medical research has told us that it works beautifully as an antidote to stress. But what's exciting about the new research is how meditation can train the mind and reshape the brain."

This fact has been borne out in studies using brain imaging techniques. For example, the brains of several Tibetan Buddhist monks were studied in 2004 while practicing loving-kindness meditation, which involved focusing on love and deep compassion for all things. The monks who were chosen had spent more than 10,000 hours practicing meditation. The result? During meditation, activity in the left medial prefrontal cortex (MPFC), the seat of positive emotions such as happiness and joy, was found to be much greater than in the right medial prefrontal cortex, where negative emotions and anxiety are located. This is something never seen before from purely mental activity (Source: *The Wall Street Journal* online, November 5, 2004). This and more recent studies show that the physical size of this part of the brain, the MPFC, of seasoned meditators is significantly larger and thicker compared to novice meditators or non-practitioners.

The Power of Attention

Scientists believe that when you disengage from "active" thinking to purposely holding loving thoughts in acute awareness, and stay there for certain periods of time, you strengthen the mental muscle represented by the left medial prefrontal cortex. This seems only logical. We know if you do curls with a weight in your hand and lift it repeatedly—up and down, up and down—on a regular basis, you strengthen the arm's physical muscle.

To date, hundreds of research studies have shown you can impact your brain and have both positive physiological as well as psychological effects as a result simply through the kind of thoughts you think. So the next time you meditate, realize you are doing something quite profound and in fact life-changing—namely creating a much more robust, flexible, and adaptable brain!

Once you are a regular practitioner of mindfulness meditation, you should begin to practice being mindful in the "active" state as well. As has been noted, this represents mindful living. It can be a difficult transition at first but a most desirable one. In other words, you can consciously transfer the deep awareness that you regularly experience in no-mind—peace, serenity, and love—into the area of everyday living. This way, you can approach the usual flurry of daily events, happenings, and occurrences with the same openness, curiosity, patience, and empathy that you experienced when you were meditating. As a result, all aspects of your life are positively impacted. In other words, you don't live in an enlightened state for just 20 or 30 minutes while meditating twice a day; you live it all the time!

Celebrities Who Meditate

Meditation in its many different forms has become popular with people from all over the world regardless of age, gender, education, occupation, language, race, social or financial standing, or faith. As such, it is a universal practice that treats a wide range of ailments and afflictions, both physical and mental, that people may have. The advantages meditation offers are many and varied. A multitude of clinical and scientific studies over the past several years have shown that the following are most common.

Meditation calms the mind and relaxes the body. In other words, a person experiences less stress, tension, and anxiety. It improves memory, concentration, and creativity. It increases open-mindedness, adaptability, and flexibility. It provides more energy, and helps control common urges and cravings such as smoking, alcohol, and drugs. It leads to better decision-making, and instills kindness, understanding, and empathy. It promotes long-term physical and mental health. Generally speaking, meditation allows a person to tap into a higher level of consciousness, and in turn experience inner peace, contentment, and a real sense of joy—all very powerful, life-enriching feelings and sensations that can be had no other way.

Obviously, you have to actually meditate on a regular basis to get these results. There is no way to fake it. For example, having lived in Europe for several years, I can attempt to explain to you what a full-bodied Italian red wine or fine, aromatic French cheese tastes like for me, when consumed either individually or together. However, you will have to taste them yourself to really understand what that experience is like for you. It's the same with meditation.

A search of the Internet lists many Hollywood celebrities who are either avid beginners or seasoned practitioners of various types of meditation. In addition to those already mentioned, these individuals include:

Jessica Alba	Jane Fonda	Katy Perry
Jennifer Aniston	Danny Glover	Keanu Reeves
Halle Berry	Herbie Hancock	Meg Ryan
Orlando Bloom	Kate Hudson	Carlos Santana
Kate Bosworth	Hugh Jackman	Martin Scorsese
Russell Brand	Angelina Jolie	Jerry Seinfeld
Adrien Brody	Patti LaBelle	Jessica Simpson
Jim Carrey	Jennifer Lopez	Will Smith
Jackie Chan	Paul McCartney	Howard Stern
Leonard Cohen	Eva Mendes	Uma Thurman
Sheryl Crowe	Kylie Minogue	Tina Turner
Clint Eastwood	Alanis Morissette	Stevie Wonder

Give some thought to this observation by Albert Einstein (1879–1955), the respected German-born theoretical physicist: "The intuitive mind is a sacred gift and the rational mind is a faithful servant. We have created a society that honors the servant but has forgotten the gift." Clearly the individuals listed here understand what Einstein knew and practiced during his long career to come up with his many remarkable discoveries.

Noble Silence

Retreats around the world offer a unique program that involves going into silence for periods of one to 40 days. The kind discussed here (although part of the Buddhist tradition, it has universal application) is called noble silence, meaning silence with full awareness. It's impossible today to find silence in the usual places: our homes, our backyards, the local park, or the beach. They have all been invaded by smartphones, iPods, iPads, tablets, laptops, TV, skate boards, loud conversations, screaming kids, booming radios, noisy cars, trucks, and motorcycles. All are examples of external stimulation run amuck. Although many retreats are often held in beautiful, isolated locations, their primary aim is to calm the mind, settle one's thoughts, establish some sort of balance or equilibrium, and perhaps offer a different perspective on life.

There are strict rules of conduct at all such retreats, although the list of do's and don'ts can vary. The don'ts often include no phones, radios, TV, Internet, iPods, iPads, e-readers, newspapers, books, magazines, cigarettes, coffee, or alcohol, and no eye or physical contact or conversation of any kind. To go and experience noble silence is definitely not a normal vacation and shouldn't be considered as such. Rather think of it as an experiential learning exercise in consciousness-awareness.

Participants have described their experience in different ways, including:

"You become more intimate with your mind and your Self."

"You get to experience another way to be."

"You come to realize that life is also about being, not only doing."

"You come to see why your normal state of mind is so messed up."

"You lose all sense of immediacy, and come to value and appreciate intimacy and relevancy a lot more."

"The present moment—Now—takes on a whole new meaning and importance."

Some claim that benefits also include positive changes in physical and mental well-being; others report a greater sense of inner strength and self-confidence, and a greater appreciation of the value and meaning of life. Considerable research over many years indicates that longevity may also be a by-product of meditation and quiet contemplation.

You may want to investigate retreats of this kind if benefits such as these, although primarily anecdotal, are of interest to you. You can find a list of those in your local area or country (indeed anywhere in the world) by searching for "spiritual retreat" or some similar term on the Internet.

Insights That Are Revealed to You While in No-Mind

If you spend all of your time—namely 100 percent—in "active" thinking and no time at all in "passive" thinking, then the following five areas will be largely unknown to you. This will have a major impact on your life, one that will lack experiencing and savoring many of the emotions that are key to positive mental health including hope, joy, wonder, love, and inner peace.

1. Forgiveness Through "Mental Cleansing"

Many experts believe that depression is the result of resistance to what is—that it is basically suppressed anger, the anger that results when you (meaning the ego) don't get what you want or expect from the world. (I agree, as this largely explains my own depressive episodes.) If so, how can you get rid of—meaning dissolve—such anger? Well, it requires forgiveness that includes forgiving both yourself and others, and fully accepting and loving what is. The goal is to be in harmony with the way things are. See the following explanation:

Your past is not something cast in concrete or etched in stone. It's only a series of memory traces that can be recalled, reanalyzed, and reinterpreted in Now and made anew. The process is called mental cleansing, and it involves taking the ego out of whatever happened to you and substituting love in its place. New information, new awareness, and a newfound sense of humility (self-love) allow you to do this. This is the way to free yourself from the bondage and pain of the past. Anger, hurt, guilt, or regret about what you did or didn't do (or what others did or didn't do) in your life up to now melt away just as the sun melts the snow. This is freedom, liberation, and enlightenment, and it opens the door to a whole new reality. It's one where you are not hurting anymore. As American author Norman Cousins (1912–1990) said, "Life is an adventure in forgiveness." This necessarily begins with forgiving yourself. We know the Buddha defined enlightenment as the end of suffering; ultimately, this is what everyone wants in life—no more suffering.

2. Beauty

True, wondrous beauty can only be appreciated while in a deep state of "pure" consciousness. In Presence. It's what you see when you don't assign mental labels. This allows you to see things directly without prior mental conditioning that only distorts and corrupts your experience. It involves stepping out of your story or personal history, detaching yourself from all your many false and erroneous beliefs and understandings, and being in the moment. In Now. You single out this very instant—this one moment in time—and recognize it as timeless and resplendent.

An example would be how you go about marveling at the beauty of a simple flower, a stately tree, a corn field, a resplendent sunset, or a bubbling brook. Do you see the tree through the clear state of "pure" awareness? Or do you see it as being only what you have previously decided a tree is, complete with a vast array of labels and misconceptions? Most people have developed a vast screen of conceptualization in the way they see everything, which in turn negates much of what is actually there including profound beauty, simple joy, and deep peace. As a result, such people end up not being able to experience these important and awe-inspiring aspects of life.

3. Passion

How do you find your passion in life? Good question! Certainly not by thinking and thinking about it, because it can come to you only through revelation, from silence, from the depths of Now. Many people look to find their passion in the world of form, then proceed to manifest what they find, again, in the world of form. The passion they find may be to accumulate great wealth, then proceed to manifest that with a fleet of expensive cars, fancy homes in exotic places, or owning a bevy of Arabian horses. This is not really a passion, of course; it's only a materialistic goal or self-serving obsession involving silly objects. It is an illusion—a fantasy, albeit of considerable proportions. Such a passion is often fueled by the ego and one that is often totally out of control. Necessarily, it leads nowhere, because all the cars, homes, and horses eventually disappear and turn into the simple dust we walk on every day. Nothing of importance or lasting significance is ever accomplished if the ego is the primary force behind your passion or your primary purpose in life.

4. Sense of Self

You cannot think your way to understanding who and what you are, to having a full, detailed, and accurate understanding of your true Nature. In other words, you cannot intellectualize or conceptualize your way to self-discovery. You are more—much more—than the thoughts you regularly engage in (actually that regularly engage you!). Such thoughts are simply the activity represented by the outer perimeter of the great wheel of life that is rotating around and around ever more rapidly. As we have seen, your essence doesn't lie on the perimeter of this circle but at the very center, that part that is firmly grounded on inner truth and not on outer circumstance. Who and what you are cannot be conceived or fully understood through conscious, "active" thinking. Only in Now, in the unlimited depths of no-mind, can you hope to gain an understanding of these factors that in turn affect every aspect of your life. Knowing this is critical. If not, you are bound to go down many unproductive and meaningless paths, and necessarily experience the frustration and pain that comes from doing that. The Now is a key consideration, and being present in Now for some time every day has to be one of your primary goals.

5. Love

Consider the question "Can you be in love without being in love?" Really the question is "Can you be in love—meaning experience selfless, sacrificial, unconditional love—without being in love romantically?" The answer? Absolutely! Here's why.

There is an inordinate and unfortunate fixation on romantic love in our society today. People chase after it, purposely and often recklessly, as though it is absolutely essential to a meaningful and happy life. But *romantic love* is only one of three different kinds of love and some would argue it is the least important of them all. The other two are: family-oriented or *familial love,* and unconditional or *transcendent love,* meaning love without thought, without preconceptions, without any judgment. These kinds of love are described in Greek in the New Testament this way: Romantic love is *eros,* familial love is *philia,* and transcendent love is *agape.*

Transcendent love by definition transcends any thought, preconceptions, or self-interest; it transcends the material world of form and can only be understood by spending time in Now. It involves loving what is at any instant in time. This really means loving life, God, or Infinite Wisdom, for this is what the Now represents. You simply single out this instant, this very second, this particular moment in time, and allow that to be your primary focus and hence your only reality.

When you sense the love that is in all things, you are never alone; you are in the company of the sacred. Transcendent love is an essential factor if you want to be a fully functioning, well-adjusted, vibrant, and interesting human being. And consider this: If familial love is not available to you, for whatever reason, and romantic love is not available to you, for whatever reason, then you'd best have transcendent love as a key part of your life. For with it, you are never alone, you are in the company of the sacred.

> "Finally, brethren, whatever things are true, whatever things
> are noble, whatever things are just, whatever things are pure,
> whatever things are lovely, whatever things are of good report,
> if there is any virtue and if there is anything praiseworthy—
> meditate on these things."
>
> —Philippians 4:8, The Apostle Paul (c. 5–c. 67 CE)

The Path to Enlightenment (Annex 10)

We think divine Presence is only an abstract concept—it isn't!

We witness it regularly—every day—all around us when we come to know profound love, pure joy, and deep peace.

There are several steps on the path to enlightenment that involve dissolving the ego and realizing the Self. Consider the following:

* ✳ We think what we see all around us in the constantly changing physical world is real. It isn't!

* ✳ We think we know who and what we are. We don't!

* ✳ We think we are separate from each other and all living things. We're not!

* ✳ We think having a lot of physical objects (stuff!) in our life will make us happy. They don't!

* We think we have no end of problems, concerns, and limitations. We don't!

* We think our mind knows best—that it knows what it should think about from minute-to-minute and day-to-day. It doesn't!

* We think the next moment is more important than the present moment. It isn't!

* We think romantic love will solve all our problems. It won't!

* We think we know the true meaning of success, happiness, and prosperity. We don't!

* We think pain and suffering are unavoidable, that they are just part of life. They're not!

* We think spending time in stillness is a waste of time. It isn't!

* We think "empty" space is just empty. It isn't!

* We think truth is found in what we believe. It isn't!

* We think it is imperative to do "something" or get "somewhere" all of the time. It isn't!

* We think the sun shines on only cloudless days. It doesn't!

The Art and Execution of Mindful Eating (Annex 11)

When you are eating, whatever you are eating, engage all your senses in the activity. All too often you eat because you are bored, unhappy, or anxious. Eating should not be an attempt to escape from a hurting mind. It should be a respectful exercise in replenishing your body and spirit.

One activity I suggest you consider seriously is mindful eating. It has many benefits, including consuming less food, better digestion, better food choices, and a more pleasant and memorable experience. In the process, you will discover that you are more than *what* you eat; you are also *how* you eat.

Assume you have a soup and sandwich for lunch. Make that tomato soup and a chicken salad sandwich (one of my favorite combinations), with iced tea. As you observe this meal on the table before you, take some time and consider what the individual items as well as the whole combination really look like. What are the colors, the smells, the shapes, the portion sizes, the way it is laid out on the table? Is the soup steaming? Does the chicken salad look sumptuous? Does the iced tea have enough ice cubes? A twisted lemon? Is your mouth beginning to water? Take a moment to take this all in before you begin to eat. And remember to give thanks.

As you proceed to eat, be mindful of each body movement in the food-consumption process. First, notice as you crank open your elbows, stretch out your arms, open your two hands, and firmly grasp the sandwich. Then notice as you slowly move the sandwich up to your mouth and your mouth toward it. Feel the anticipation (as you salivate) of the very first bite.

As you eagerly open your mouth and bite into the food, what does that feel like? What sounds are created? What tastes do you experience first? Are there other ones you can discern in the background? How is each one different? Strong, medium, or mellow? What spices or chopped vegetables can you identify? Parsley? Onion? Celery? What is the texture of the chicken salad? Is it firm, creamy, and crunchy? Or soft, bland, and mushy?

As you proceed to chew the food a few more times, what new tastes or sensations do you experience? What kind of bread have you chosen? How does it affect the overall taste? Is the bread toasted? (No? Why not?) How does the occasional spoonful of hot tomato soup change the experience? Add or subtract? How does the occasional sip of cold iced tea change the experience? Add or subtract? Is the whole exercise beginning to diminish your hunger pains? Are you already thinking about what you want for dessert? Ice cream? Vanilla or chocolate? Two scoops or one? Or does the New York cheesecake have special appeal?

This is just the beginning of how you can involve your mind, body, and senses while you are eating. If you are at a restaurant, you can add noticing the surroundings inside the room itself—its colors, brightness, size, and shape; the windows—their size, contours, and shape; the wall coverings—any interesting photos or paintings; the ceiling—light fixtures, color, and contour; and the floor—is it wood, tile, or carpeting? Is the floor clean? And what does the room temperature feel like—too hot, too cold, or just right?

Are other customers in attendance? How many? How are they dressed? How old, how young? Any couples? Any children? Quiet or noisy? How many people are at each table? What are the size and shape of the other tables? Are the napkins paper or cloth? Tablecloths? And what food and drinks have they ordered? (Maybe you missed the daily special!) Are there any other colors, smells, or sounds in the background (i.e., music such as country, pop, hard/soft rock, or classical; the banging of plates, glasses, or tableware)? Oops! Almost forgot. How comfortable is your chair? Is the seat hard or soft? Too low or too high? Is it made of wood, plastic, or metal? Does it have arm-rests? Is it old or new? Now consider how all this comes together to determine your overall experience of this occasion.

Okay. You have just had an enjoyable lunch. You put food in your mouth 21 times. You chewed each mouthful at least 15 times. You then swallowed each mouthful as well. (Right? Either that or you still have food in your mouth!) The soup was lukewarm before you finished it. All the ice had melted in your glass. And the whole exercise took about one hour. (That's an average of 2.8 minutes between each swallow.) Perhaps we'd best move on before the six-course dinner arrives; that could take all evening!

"The moment one gives close attention to anything, even a blade of grass, it becomes a mysterious, awesome, indescribably magnificent world in itself."

—Arthur Miller (1915–2005),
American playwright and essayist;
and author of *Death of a Salesman* (1949)

You at Your Essence are "Pure" Consciousness (Annex 12)

Every sage from every age has said the following: On the physical level, you are an expression of the Divine; at the deepest level, you are the Divine.

Let's dissect Presence (i.e., stillness) with a very sharp scalpel to find its constituent parts. In the physical world, the world of form, this is easy enough to do. Consider a miner looking to see what precious metals (gold/silver) are hidden in the rocks he has just uncovered.

The objective is to slow your thoughts down to zero, or as close to zero as possible, through mindfulness meditation. With your eyes open, begin to shift your attention to your breath. Slowly breathe in, breathe out: count *one*; breathe in, breathe out: count *two*; continue up to 25. As you do this, you can note what your senses perceive in your immediate surroundings. For example, consider the room you are in. What do you see, what do you hear, and what do you smell? A main feature of any physical setting is always the huge amount of so-called "empty" space that is all around you.

For example, the people, the furniture, the pictures, the curtains, the rugs, and all the other trappings probably make up less than 5 percent of that whole space. (Of course empty space is also a key aspect of things both very big and very small, from the ever-expanding cosmos down to the tiny atom.) Now, as you continue to focus on this empty space, something interesting begins to happen: *You start to think a little less.* You pay less attention to the usual problems, concerns, and preoccupations that your mind usually entertains and from which it gets its (often-negative) energy.

Next, shift your attention inward to your physical body. Begin to sense the energy and aliveness that are there. It could be sensations regarding your neck, shoulders, arms, chest, back, legs, or feet, and it may range from a slight tingling to a certain stiffness or lingering pain. One way to proceed is to close your eyes and consider how you know that your body exists. What is it that tells you your body is actually there? Again, as you do this, *your thinking continues to slow down.* You are less affected by the stream of compulsive thoughts that usually dominate your conscious awareness. Fewer thoughts in turn allow you to relax: Your blood pressure falls, your heartbeat slows down, your breathing is slower and deeper, and your skin and muscles are much less tense. The relaxation response has been activated.

What else do you find when attempting to see what makes up the present moment? As we have just seen, there are the "outer" aspects you can sense and the "inner" aspects you can feel. And of course, as you do this, there is always a stream of pesky, irritating thoughts lingering in the background, all frantically waiting to be recognized. Yes, they appear less and less, but their very presence exposes something else. Together they show that there is a small space in time between when one thought comes and leaves, and when the next one arrives. This is something quite remarkable: a gap in time in which *no thoughts* are generated—in which *nothing* is being experienced.

This may be the first time in your life that you experienced a short pause in your thinking that you actually noticed. You were able to slow down the thoughts in your mind enough to see that one comes, then goes, another one comes, then goes, etc. They come only one at a time, each seeking your prompt attention, and each with a small space between them that represents unconditioned or "pure" consciousness. This is the deepest level, the very essence of Now. And, it is also *your* essence. Psalm 46:10 says, "Be still, and know that I am God." Yes, God or deep peace or infinite wisdom is found in stillness, in the depths of Now.

It's important to know that this space cannot be accurately described, enhanced, understood, or duplicated any other way. It's singular; it stands alone as the Source of all that is. Strangely enough, you don't even know when you are actually in the gap, for as soon as you realize you are "there," you are not there anymore. You are back again in conscious awareness, thinking, wondering, and marveling at what just happened.

Now, as you begin to understand how the mind works, you come to realize something quite profound: You are a detached witness to the intimate workings of your mind, to all the thoughts it entertains. In other words, *you notice you are aware that you are aware.* But you also quickly realize that you are not what you are aware of, namely your thoughts, your emotions, your surroundings, your body, your plans, or your activities. You are not these transient, inconsequential, and superficial things. Rather you are the intelligence or deep *knowing* that allows you to be aware of such things!

So we see that the primary, dominant feature of both the physical and mental worlds is empty space. And this space allows you to be aware that you are aware. This is where you participate in and celebrate life; you are an innocent, detached observer of everything that you ever think, see, hear, feel, say, and do. You are the silent watcher watching the watcher. Of course you may be imperfect or broken in the way you do some of these things—we all are—but "you" in your essence are not broken at all because these things are not you! You are the space in conscious awareness in which everything happens; you are not what happens.

Amazing! Through the process of calming your mind, you can sense your own presence, your own existence, your own essence. Of course it isn't "yours" per se; it is the collective presence of all living things, the "One" consciousness of which we are all a part. At last! You know who you are. This is the precise moment of enlightenment.

You need to know how significant this realization is. You are not your thoughts, your beliefs, your feelings, your successes, your failures, your hopes, or your fears; you are not your upbringing, your relationships, your occupation, or your education. You are not what you have ever thought, believed, experienced, felt, said, or done. In short, you are not your elaborate and ever-expanding "story." Why? Because you are consciousness itself.

There is a space in you that involves no thinking. It may last for only a second or two or three—the duration is immaterial—yet its presence is immensely significant. First, it reveals to you what you are not, namely the musings and mutterings going on in your mind. Second, this space, being a higher level of consciousness, is able to reveal to you things about yourself and your world that can be had no other way. This includes the fact that you at your core are unconditional, transcendent love. And third, spending time in this space allows you to have a wider and more informed perspective on how to deal with the many challenges and opportunities you face in your everyday life, both personal and professional. For example, it allows you to respond with wisdom and caring to events and happenings when otherwise you would react to them with haste and detachment.

In summary, when you access the stillness in you, you discover the following: The *stillness* in you is the "it" of the Universe; the *awareness* in you is the "it" of the Universe; the *knower* in you is the "it" of the Universe. The "it" and you are one and the same. Your "is-ness" is also Now's "is-ness." You are part of a much greater whole. Now, by exploring this dimension in all of its wondrous and illuminating breadth and depth, you are able to commune with the Divine.

"It takes a little time to create a gap between the witness and the mind. Once the gap is there, however, you are in for a great surprise—namely that you are not the mind, that you are the witness, a watcher."

—Chandra Mohan Jain (1931–1990),
Indian Mystic and Spiritual Teacher

"You yourself, as much as anybody in the entire universe, deserve your love and affection."

—Siddhartha Gautama (c. 563–483 BCE),
Indian prince and Spiritual Master;
founder of Buddhism

"Twenty years from now, you will be more disappointed by the things you did not do than the things you did."

—Mark Twain (1835–1910),
American humorist, satirist, lecturer, and writer;
author of *The Adventures of Huckleberry Finn* (1884)

"Formulate and stamp indelibly on your mind a mental picture of yourself as succeeding. Hold this picture tenaciously. Never permit it to fade. Your mind will seek to develop the picture."

—Dr. Norman Vincent Peale (1898–1993),
American Protestant preacher;
author of *The Power of Positive Thinking* (1952)

Knowing About Practical Spirituality

"During the past 30 years, people from all the civilized countries of the earth have consulted me. Many hundreds of patients have passed through my hands. Among all my patients in the second half of life—that is to say, over 35— there has not been one whose problem in the last resort was that of not finding a religious outlook on life. It is safe to say that every one of them fell ill because he had lost what the living religions of every age have given to their followers, and none of them has been really healed who did not regain his religious outlook."

—Carl Jung (1875–1961),
Swiss psychiatrist and psychotherapist;
author of *The Undiscovered Self* (1957)

**P
A
R
T

5**

Are You Making Progress?

There are three ways to know if you are making any progress on the spiritual path:

1. The extent to which you don't think,

2. The extent to which you have taken the ego out of your thinking, and

3. The extent to which you are at peace.

"Learn to get in touch with the silence within yourself, and know that everything in life has a purpose. There are no mistakes, no coincidences, all events are blessings given to us to learn from."

> —Elizabeth Kubler-Ross, MD (1926–2004),
> Swiss-American psychiatrist and researcher;
> author of *On Death and Dying* (1969)

Practical Spirituality

"Lives of great men all remind us

We can make our lives sublime,

And, departing, leave behind us

Footprints on the sand of time."

> —Henry Wadsworth Longfellow (1807–1882),
> American poet and educator;
> author of "The Song of Hiawatha" (1855)

The following represents a compilation of ideas, concepts, and insights from the many lectures and seminars I have given and the books and essays I have written over the past 25 years. Together, they represent a guide to positive, peaceful, and purposeful living, one that is centered in the stillness and joy of our authentic selves. With this as your solid base, you will be able to live a dynamic, fulfilling, and spiritually oriented life, one of your own choosing yet one that is also chosen for you by God.

Spirituality is not served well by language of any kind; indeed, no serious subject is. All language originates from the world of form and hence necessarily has limitations contained within it. For example, how accurately and meaningfully could you explain to another person what a latte or a peanut butter cookie really tastes like, whether consumed individually or indeed together? Or consider winning a gold medal at the Olympics, successfully climbing Mount Everest, or falling madly in love. When people in these situations are asked, "How does it feel?" they usually respond by saying something like, "It's an incredible feeling but I really can't put it into words. It has to be experienced."

We in the West in particular are all too quick to put labels on everything we see and experience—another compulsion of the mind—and this can only lead to serious misunderstandings and unnecessary complications. Isn't it strange, and arrogant of us, that at the precise moment we put a label on something, we think we *know* it? I suggest you strongly resist this temptation and trust instead in your own ability to experience true awareness, understanding, peace, joy, bliss, and love on their own terms.

1 You are being asked in this book, perhaps for the very first time in your life, to analyze in detail how you actually *think*. All too often you spend a lot of time thinking in small, concentric circles (i.e., from A to F!) about why you are not living the kind of life you want to be living, not doing what you want to be doing, and not getting the results you want to be getting. You are stuck in a pattern of thinking that is getting you nowhere, certainly not ahead, yet you don't know what to do to break free. You are locked in limbo, frozen in place, confined to a prison of your own making. It seems the best you can do is to ask this important question: "Where is the key, because I want to get out of here?"

But how could this happen? Invariably, at some point in your life, you will find that things are not progressing the way you think they should. You are disillusioned with life and unable to bridge the gap between wanting something and doing something in order to have it. Faced with this difficulty, you accept you have to confront head-on personal failure and growing frustration. Clearly you understand your feelings about your predicament but are at a loss what to do about them. After all, having ongoing feelings of disappointment and despair is not exactly conducive to taking decisive action.

As you read through this book, you are going to discover the following: You must embark on a journey of introspection and self-assessment to discover your true source of inspiration. The process involves coming to a well-informed conclusion about who and what you are, and why you're here. As you travel down this road, you will find that buried memories will come alive again, and bring renewed energy and excitement back into your life. In turn, you will become alive again as well.

If you agree to engage in this activity, the rewards you'll receive will be in direct proportion to the amount of effort—time, energy, curiosity, and open-mindedness—you invest in the process. The good news is that even a mind that is seemingly hard-wired (meaning very closed to change) can be modified if sufficient interest, determination, and persistence are present.

2 Life is one long continuum of activity. Inertia lies at one end of the scale, and it creates monotony, sadness, and misery in your life; action lies at the other end, and it creates excitement, happiness, and fulfillment in your life. The ideas in this text are designed to specifically minimize the former and maximize the latter. Our analysis will necessarily lead to the thoughts you are thinking on an ongoing basis and the feelings they generate. These feelings in turn are a prime indicator of the quality of thinking you are engaged in as well as the quality of life you are enjoying.

Consider the following:

Assume an exciting, inspirational thought strikes you: "I'd like to be an entrepreneur (or an engineer, a scientist, a doctor, a nurse, a journalist, a history professor, a business executive...). I have lots of good ideas. The newspapers are full of stories all the time about people who have succeeded at starting a new business. It sure would be exciting to try."

You then say: "But who am I to think I could succeed? I don't have what it takes. I don't have the education, the experience, the network of people, the necessary financing, the skills, the determination—and I'm not the smartest person in the world, that's for sure." In other words, without any serious thought on your part, you quickly evaluate the possibility of succeeding at a certain endeavor, and conclude you are neither capable nor deserving.

You then feel: Sad, down, perhaps even a bit depressed. All the fears and doubts you ever had rise once again to the surface and reinforce your evaluation of yourself. You quickly retreat back into your comfort zone (aka the dead zone) where you know it's safe.

Here, there is no pressure on you. You don't have to prove anything to anyone, including yourself. You just accept the low opinion you have of yourself; it's the path of least resistance. After all, no one knows you better than you know yourself, so obviously your evaluation of yourself and your prospects for success are correct. (Wrong!) The result? You are immobilized, and your feelings of self-doubt and lack of confidence keep you exactly where you are. As a result, nothing in your life changes very much, including your low opinion of yourself.

This thought sequence plays itself out in the minds of thousands, if not millions, of people all over the world every day. On the surface, the conclusion that is reached appears quite logical; on closer scrutiny, however, it does not. There is simply no conclusive evidence to support it, no matter who the individual is. Any belief you may have about yourself and your abilities to succeed at any activity needs to be tested in the real world through action—and often repeated action—and experience. It begins and ends with two four-letter words: hard work. (Recall Thomas Edison's comment that genius is 1 percent inspiration and 99 percent perspiration.)

3 We get up in the morning, groom our physical bodies, don our physical clothes, and satisfy our physical hunger. We proceed to go to some physical place, and compete and compare by playing silly games in the confines of our physical world to receive primarily physical rewards. At a certain level, we wonder why we do this all the time. Is this what we have been created to do? Is this all there is to our Being? Is this all a silly dream and we need to awaken from it? If so, how?

4One moment of insight is more valuable than a lifetime of experience. So consider the following and what insight you might gain from it.

People generally experience a wide variety of feelings as they go about each day, accompanied by a corresponding level of stress and anxiety. These feelings can range from simple discouragement and disappointment in some cases (i.e., low reaction) to desperation and despair in other cases (i.e., high reaction). If intense enough, the latter can lead to extreme anxiety, or even moderate to severe depression. Let's look more closely at this ailment, depression, for it can have serious consequences if not diagnosed early and dealt with promptly.

Depression is the manifestation or emotional response to an observed incongruence between what you are currently experiencing (i.e., the thoughts/cognitions you are having, and how you are interpreting and internalizing them) on a day-to-day basis, called your "actual" reality or reality one, and what you want and think you should be experiencing (i.e., events, happenings, or outcomes), what is called your "preferred" reality or reality two. This apparent dichotomy often takes place at both the conscious and subconscious level.

Depression, which could be accompanied by feelings of extreme sadness and despair and acts of aggression, will continue to haunt you in your life until you come to understand that both reality one and reality two are rooted totally in the ego, meaning your limited and inaccurate sense of self. It is the ego that distorts and manipulates your thinking, and in turn causes emotional upheaval and distress that in extreme cases can lead to thoughts about death and suicide.

This in part explains the huge increase in interest in practical spirituality in our society today. For it is through spirituality that you come to see that both reality one and reality two are illusions. Hence both are irrelevant and meaningless, which means that the perceived difference between them is irrelevant and meaningless as well. Such realities are simply imperfect mental constructs based on false assumptions and erroneous beliefs, and a serious lack of understanding about how the mind works.

It all comes down to seeing and appreciating the role the "one Self" plays regarding human consciousness and awareness as compared to the role the individual little self or ego plays. The former is accommodating, accepting, and inclusive; the latter is competitive, confrontational, and exclusive. A clear understanding of who and what you are is known as reality three, and it is the only constant, true reality. How close you come to living out this reality on a daily basis is indicative of how close you have come to being awakened and enlightened, and experiencing the joy and peace that this brings into your life.

Understanding how your delusions can confuse, trick, and restrict you in your thinking has huge implications not only for your own behavior but for the behavior of groups, organizations, and society at large. This topic is related to what is called self-image psychology, which in turn deals with the three key elements of the human psyche, namely (1.) the self-concept, (2.) the self-image, and (3.) self-esteem. The latter, self-esteem—how much you truly like, love, value, or esteem yourself—determines to a large extent how you live your life: your relationships; your work and career; your accomplishments, both personal and professional; and your physical, mental, and emotional health. Together, these determine the quality of your life in all its many and magnificent manifestations.

5 "Ego-speak" is the playing out of thoughts in your mind that represent your basic fears and desires, all the things you think you need to complete what you perceive as your faulty and limited sense of self. For example, do you want to be important? The ego will gladly show you how. Do you want to impress others? Again, the ego will gladly show you how. But consider this: After the ego has shown you myriad ways to be important, impress others, and show others how smart, how successful, and how special you are, what have you really accomplished? Why do you feel you have to do this all the time? What other important experiences in life are you missing out on because of this constant preoccupation, this unrelenting obsession? Which part of you is doing all the doubting about your real self-worth here?

6The following is a traditional Native American story that has been passed down over many years, titled "Two Wolves": "An old Cherokee chief is teaching his grandson about life. 'A fight is going on inside me,' he said to the boy. 'It is a terrible fight and it's between two wolves. One is evil—he is anger, envy, sorrow, regret, greed, arrogance, self-pity, guilt, resentment, inferiority, lies, false pride, superiority, self-doubt, and ego. The other is good—he is joy, peace, love, hope, serenity, humility, kindness, benevolence, empathy, generosity, truth, compassion, and faith.' The grandson thought about this for a moment and then asked, 'Grandfather, which wolf will win?' The old chief simply replied, 'The one you continue to feed.'"

7You shouldn't be surprised or alarmed that unexpected and unwanted events (usually viewed as problems or setbacks) will continue to occur in your life, despite your best efforts to avoid them. They are simply part of life's journey. They can, in fact, be extremely helpful.

If you find yourself in a situation that is causing you ongoing pain and suffering, it's simply telling you that you are not in tune with your spirit, with who you are. I believe God has a plan for each of us, and sometimes He needs to send us a wake-up call that says, "Hey, I know you are hurting, so don't forget about me!" We may hear this call on a specific occasion or it could be a constant, gentle whisper that never goes away. We need to know our Father doesn't want to hurt us, He wants to heal us; He doesn't want to punish us, He wants to protect us (usually from ourselves!). He is forever wanting reunion with His creations and His voice will not go unheard. In this way, unwanted events, even extremely tragic ones, can be blessings in disguise because they bring us back to the path, back to His perfect plan.

8In the minds of some, there seems to be a great deal of confusion regarding "knowing about" God versus "knowing" God. You can come to know "about God" by reading the scriptures or other religious books on the topic and going to church, a temple, a mosque, or synagogue. "Knowing" God, however, and practicing His ways as a way of life is a very different matter and involves a very different process.

It's like the difference between a map and the actual territory. A map is not the territory; it's only someone's two-dimensional approximation of what that territory is like. You can never get to "know" God by reading a book about God, or going to church and listening to someone speak about God, no matter how good that book is or how knowledgeable and eloquent that speaker is. Similarly, you can never get to "know" the Grand Canyon by studying a map about the Grand Canyon or listening to someone speak about the Grand Canyon, no matter how good that map is or how knowledgeable that speaker is.

The proof of whether you "know" God or not is simple: Have you adopted His ways as your ways in your everyday life? Are you God-like in your thoughts, feelings, and actions? Do you live according to God's teachings or simply to further your own personal agenda?

9 Light travels at 186,000 miles per second. Moving at this speed, it would take a person exactly 1.284 seconds to arrive at the moon, as it is 238,857 miles away. That's about the time it takes you to snap your fingers. While traveling at this same speed, however, it would take a person *2.3 million years* to get to the galaxy nearest to Earth! (This means you would arrive with very long fingernails and in desperate need of a haircut!) It's called Andromeda. And we know there are thousands upon thousands of other galaxies billions of light-years beyond that (Source: Wikipedia). Clearly the Infinite is not only stranger than we think it is, it's stranger than we can think!

10 You may wonder at the slow pace of human evolution. Why are we so ignorant about so many things? Why can't we seem to get along with each other? Why do envy, distrust, and hatred still abound in relationships among individuals, groups, and nation states? Why does it seem we are incapable of loving our neighbors as well as ourselves? Richard Christopher Carrington (1826–1875), an English amateur astronomer, puts it all in perspective with this explanation:

> "Let us imagine that, by some magic, the whole Earth's history could be compressed into a single year. On this scale, the first eight months would be completely without life. The following two would be devoted to the most primitive of creatures. No mammals would appear until the second week in December. Man, as we know him, would strut onto the stage at approximately 11:45 p.m. on December 31. The age of written history would occupy little more than the last 60 seconds on the clock."

Can you imagine that? In this analogy, we see that we've been around for *only 15 minutes* in a full year that has 525,600 minutes in it! It's obvious our species is still in its infancy. Yet we have to wonder if and when we will ever grow up. (Hmmm. Is there something you can do in the meantime to help facilitate this?)

Although precise numbers are still being debated, scientists generally agree that our universe was formed about 13.7 billion years ago; that planet Earth was formed about 4.6 billion years ago, that the first elementary life forms appeared on Earth about 3.8 billion years ago, that early dinosaurs roamed the planet about 230 million years ago, that human history began about 7 million years ago, and that homo erectus appeared about 1.7 million years ago (Source: Wikipedia).

11 Consider *neurosis*. Neurosis is a mental disorder that describes any number of emotional disturbances that may include stress, anxiety, compulsions, obsessions, insecurity, anger, paranoia, depression, or guilt, as well as fears and phobias of various kinds. It's generally the result of a distorted, inaccurate, or irrational perception of reality. Anyone seeking a cure for this affliction must begin by realizing, first, that such pain and suffering are always self-inflicted (no one can cause you to feel anything; you always choose to feel the way you do, whether consciously or unconsciously); and second, that such pain always has its origins in the cognitions (the thoughts and the interconnectedness of thoughts) being practiced by the individual. The road to wellness is always to critically analyze and question the original thoughts and thought sequences themselves. This will lead you directly to the source of any suffering you may be experiencing (again, say hello to the ego!).

The fact is, everyone is a neurotic to some extent. No one perceives the world 100 percent correctly, no one thinks 100 percent correctly, and no one ever will. The critical question then becomes, "Are your current neuroses so debilitating that they are preventing you from being a happy and productive person in all the ways you want to be happy and productive?" If so, you need to do something about it.

A neurotic person needlessly inflicts pain on himself by engaging in faulty and erroneous thinking. In other words, such a person injures himself both mentally and physically for reasons that are totally not necessary.

For example, a neurotic typically practices a particular manner of thinking over and over again, yet knows there is no possibility of a different outcome. The person's illogical and irrational thoughts are simply being cycled and recycled, resulting in only more intense and deeper feelings of misery and worthlessness. For some, this type of repetitive thinking may give temporary relief. They bask in the illusion, at least for a time, that they are making progress because they are engaged in some kind of mental activity. Eventually, however, it only creates more anxiety because they soon come to realize they are right back where they started. (One definition of insanity is when someone does the same thing over and over again, yet still expects a different outcome. Using this as our gauge, how sane/insane are you?)

Imagine you are an airplane on the ground that wants to take off, but you don't know how. So you just taxi around the airport hour after hour thinking it's bound to happen sooner or later. After all, you are an airplane! You *are* meant to fly! All this effort is frustrating, time-consuming, and very nauseating, of course. It keeps you in the same place—a sort of living hell. And in a real sense, it is fatal. It drains you of your creativity, it eats away at your self-confidence, and eventually it kills your dream (i.e., at some point, you will run out of gas!).

This is not a discussion about aeronautics, however. It is about going beyond inertia and the misery it creates in your life to personal empowerment and experiencing the fulfillment you really want in your life. It is about breaking free from your past and creating a whole new future. It may sound silly but this book is about following your dream, doing your thing, being true to who and what you are. It is about being who you can and must be, and doing what you can and must do, often for seemingly selfish but, in fact, altruistic reasons.

12 Here is a quote from the book *Inner Peace, Inner Power* (1985) by Dr. Nelson Boswell that gives further insight into how we think:

> "Whether we are neurotic or not, we believe what we tell ourselves is reality, but often we come up with falsehoods, incomplete information, half-truths, and sometimes even nonsense. Our conclusions are often slightly or grossly slanted. We go around programming ourselves with our inner statements and messages, and we don't even hear ourselves. We don't sense the full meaning of what we say. We're not even aware that it is we who are programming our own minds. And then, when we're feeling down, angry, bitter or hopeless, we are not aware that it had to happen. We brought it upon ourselves...."

13 It shouldn't be any surprise that anxiety (which in turn often generates fear and trepidation) is so prevalent in our society today. Most of us live simply by trial and error, a sure recipe for disappointment and despair. Consider the following manner of thinking in which most people are engaged. First, you know you can't predict the future, and some bad things will invariably happen to you that you have no control over. *Yikes!* Second, you are unhappy with some things from your past and aren't able to change any of them. *Yikes!* And third, you are a phony. You are acting in your life as though you know who you are when, in fact, you don't. You have no idea. In addition, it seems your deception will soon be discovered by those who know you well. *Yikes!* I'd be anxious, too, if I thought this way.

14 Any peace process among individuals, groups, or nations should follow these basic steps: (1) actively engage, (2) seek to understand, (3) practice acceptance, and (4) offer unconditional love. The alternative is to confront, bully, repudiate, or even try to exterminate. This results in you digging your grave and the other side digging theirs. Bravo! Another win for the ego and yet another loss for humankind.

15 Here is a quote from the book *The Magic in Your Mind* (1961) by American author U.S. Andersen. It demonstrates an incredible degree of insight into what we are talking about:

> "We exist in order that we may become something more than we are, not through favorable circumstance or auspicious occurrence, but through an inner search for increased awareness. To be, to become, these are the commandments of evolving life, which is going somewhere, aspires to some unscaled heights, and the awakened soul answers the call, seeks, grows, expands. To do less is to sink into the reactive prison of the ego, with all its pain, suffering, limitation, decay, and death. The man who lives through reaction to the world about him is the victim of every change in his environment, now happy, now sad, now victorious, now defeated, affected but never affecting. He may live many years in this manner, rapt with sensory perception and the ups and downs of his surface self, but one day pain so outweighs pleasure that he suddenly perceives his ego as illusory, a product of outside circumstances only. Then he either sinks into complete animal lethargy or, turning away from the senses, seeks inner awareness and self-mastery. Then he

is on the road to really living, truly becoming; then he begins to uncover his real potential; then he discovers the miracle of his own consciousness, the magic in his mind."

16 The role the ego plays in your life is critical to understand, for the ego can cause you no end of grief if left unnoticed and unchecked. I would go this far on the matter and state the following:

The ego in you lies at the center of what causes all the pain and suffering you will ever experience in your life.

The curse of the ego as it affects human behavior has been noted and written about for centuries. In more recent times, William Shakespeare (1564–1616) incorporated this fact into the plot of many of his plays. It was also highlighted by American poet and essayist T.S. Eliot (1888–1965) when he commented, "Most of the trouble in the world is caused by people wanting to be important." And Gelek Rimpoche, a Michigan-based Tibetan Buddhist lama and author of *Good Life, Good Death* (2001), went even further when he said, "The true enemy is inside. The maker of trouble, the source of all our suffering, the destroyer of our joy, and the destroyer of our virtue, is inside. It is EGO." (emphasis in original)

If you fail to understand the ego and how it impacts, distorts, and manipulates your thinking, you will experience pain in many aspects of your life. If you feel you want to engage in a heated debate about this statement, it's only because the ego in you is feeling threatened and wants to leap to its own defense! I implore you to deny it this opportunity. In the meantime, keep an open mind on the matter and see if your view changes over time.

What is the ego, anyway? Where does it come from? What does it do, both positive and negative, productive and unproductive? These are key questions you must answer if you want to understand how you function and why you so often fail at, or at least fall short of, being who you are and achieving the peace of mind you want.

The ego is defined as self-centered, self-importance, self-conceit, self-absorption. It originates from the Greek word meaning "little, separated self," as opposed to the collective "one Self."

We know the ego is something that our species created over several million years of evolution; as well, you have come to believe it is an essential part of who you are and that it has your best interests in mind. (Wrong!) In other words, you think it represents the *real* you. This belief or mindset is based on the erroneous assumption that you are separate from everything and everyone else; that you need to look after, protect, and nurture yourself in competition with, and exclusion of, everyone else; and that as an individual, you are somehow special, meaning more worthy, more deserving, and more important (and all that this entails) than everyone else.

The ego in you is a very busy fellow, working tirelessly night and day with only one goal in mind: to masquerade as your best friend and protector, all the while keeping you separate from your true Nature, your Source, the collective consciousness of all that is. This is a master deception—in fact, the ultimate deception of all human existence: that you are alone and separate, and hence vulnerable, and can survive and prosper only if you put your interests first, well ahead of everyone else.

17 Consider the question "Where are you looking for meaning?" The vast majority of people look for the most important things they want in life—acceptance, love, prosperity, health, happiness, peace of mind, meaning, and personal fulfillment—*outside* themselves. Let's give these attributes a specific name. Let's call them high-level spiritual needs. People look and look and look, but don't really find what they are looking for. So they end up disappointed and frustrated, even angry both with themselves and others. This leads them to ask some serious questions: "What's wrong? Why isn't life giving me all that I want? Am I not capable, worthy, and deserving?"

You have been taught, through social conditioning and environmental programming, to believe—again wrongly—that you can find what you want in life outside yourself. This is another paradigm, literally a framework or mental construct, which is a certain way of thinking to which you have become accustomed. As such, it is firmly ingrained in your mind and won't easily go away.

At first glance, it does seem logical to look at what you can actually see that is physically all around you for all the things you want. After all, this stuff is right there, right in front of you. You can clearly see it, you can often touch and sometimes even taste it, and you can easily relate to it and earnestly want it. But alas, what you see is only an illusion, a temporary state of affairs that is constantly changing, constantly evolving. Of course, physical things that you can see and touch are always "transforming."

The problem is most acute when you continue to look to the physical world to define your Self, to determine who and what you are. For example, you may say to yourself and others, "*I am what I do.* I am a teacher, a laborer, a truck driver, an accountant, a homemaker"; or you may say, "*I am what I own.* I am my car, my clothes, my jewelry, my bank account, my house"; or you may say, "*I am my body.* I am my skin, my lips, my eyes, my legs, my hair."

But you would be wrong in each and every case. Who you are has nothing to do with the physical world. The world at large has no idea who you are; that isn't its job. It's yours! And once you understand this, you'd better wise up and look in another place, in another direction—say, *inside* yourself. After all, if what you want in life cannot be found "out there," the only other place to look is "in here!"

18 *Materialism* is the doctrine that says physical things and physical matter (all that is in form) are the only true reality, and that everything else in the world, including thought, will, spirit, love, insight, and wisdom, can be explained and interpreted only in terms of matter; it's the belief that comfort, wealth, power, pleasure, and success are the only and the highest goals you should strive for; it's the tendency to be more concerned in life with material things and physical objects than with spiritual thoughts that instill feelings of joy, wonder, hope, serenity, and deep peace.

Why do we, especially in the West, immerse ourselves in a culture of materialism? Is it just another form of escapism? If so, from what are we trying to escape? Some would say we are escaping from accepting our divinity because if we accepted it, we'd have to live up to it—and most people aren't prepared to do that. Why are we individually and collectively such willing participants? What are we accomplishing by participating (in many cases, indulging) in this? Why do we encourage our children to go down the same path? Is it that we don't know any better? Are we simply involved in perpetuating the silly game called "monkey-see, monkey-do," and just let the game go on?

Our preoccupation with the physical world, with what we can perceive with our five senses, is a major problem for society today. Why? Because you cannot get what you want most in life through the frantic and uncontrolled accumulation of more and more things! On your deathbed, do you plan to brag about how many pairs of expensive shoes you bought during your lifetime, how many juicy lobster tails you ate, how many bottles of premium wine you drank, or how much you paid for your favorite putter or driver?

19 The following strictures indicate how several of the world's major religions view excessive consumption:

* Buddhism: "By the thirst for the riches, the foolish man destroys himself as if he were his own enemy."

* Christianity: "Watch out! Be on your guard against all kinds of greed; a person's life does not consist of an abundance of possessions."

* Confucianism: "Excess and deficiency are equally at fault."

* Hinduism: "When you have the golden gift of commitment, you have everything."

* Islam: "It is difficult for a person laden with riches to climb the steep path that leads to bliss."

❈   Taoism: "One who knows he or she has enough is rich."

(Source: Douglas V. Smith and Kazi F. Jalal)

20 Pierre Teillard de Chardin (1881–1955), the French theologian and paleontologist, made this interesting statement: *"You are not a human being having a spiritual experience; you are a spiritual being having a human experience."*

Think about it. Have you ever bruised a knee? Have you ever scratched an itch? Do you regularly cut your hair? Do you regularly trim your fingernails? Have you ever bled from a cut? Have you ever suffered from a sun-burn? Have you ever broken a bone? Have you ever hungered for food or water? Yes? Then you are human.

Alternately, have you ever been sad? Have you ever been happy? Have you ever cried? Have you ever laughed? Have you ever been a voluntary giver and felt great? Have you ever been a voluntary receiver and felt grateful? Have you ever regretted something you did? Have you ever hungered for love and basked in being loved? Yes? Then you are spirit.

As spirit, you necessarily have a number of needs that you are striving to satisfy. You want to love and be loved; you want to accept and be accepted, to have hope, happiness, peace of mind, fulfillment, meaning, and a real sense of purpose. You want to feel worthy, to be relevant, to know in your heart and soul that you are important. Nothing more, nothing less.

So a question. How many of us are spending all of our time and energy trying to satisfy our spiritual needs from a physical world? The answer: *practically all of us!* But it's obvious a physical world is incapable of satisfying spiritual needs. Think about it. How much can a rock love you, even if it is a three-carat diamond? It cannot. Or a mansion in Hollywood? Or a Ferrari? Or a Rolex? Or a private Lear jet? The physical world mocks us with the phrase "Seek me out and you will find." But this is an illusion. We have to look *inside*—at our very essence, our spirit, our Godliness, you might say—to meet our most important needs.

21 As a species, we have been very successful at exploiting technology, especially in the last few hundred years. Sir Isaac Newton, the English mathematician, alchemist, and philosopher, introduced the world to the scientific method, namely how to discover so-called "reality" by using rational, logical, linear, left-brain thought, with reality meaning "what actually is," including how the universe works. The many marvels that our minds have come up with are almost too numerous to mention: television, jet aircraft, nuclear reactors, spacecraft, the computer, cell phones, solar energy, the Internet, and so forth.

Is our proven prowess to mold our environment to our liking, leading us to believe that we can solve all of our problems ourselves? Albert Einstein once commented that humans cannot hope to solve all the problems they have created by using the same mind that created them. Take a moment and think about this, as it may apply to you and your so-called "problems."

Newton lived from 1642 to 1727. It has been said that he discovered more of the essential core of human knowledge than anyone before or after. Chet Raymo, a U.S. science columnist and author of *The Path: A One-Mile Walk Through the Universe* (2003), has said this of Newton:

> "He developed the theory of infinite series, and showed that it was possible to treat the Infinite and the Infinitesimal with mathematical rigor. He refined concepts of space, time, inertia, force, momentum, and acceleration, and formulated laws of mechanical motion. He invented the Theory of Universal Gravitation and applied it to celestial and terrestrial motions. To facilitate his calculations, he devised what is now called the differential and integral calculus."

Note that Newton accomplished all this before he was 24 years old!

Incredibly intelligent people such as Newton don't come along very often. But even Newton was unable to explain where matter originated or who/what devised all the laws of physics and mathematics in the first place. Clearly, we are sadly lacking in our ability to fully understand and master the physical world.

For example, man has never created something from nothing. Think about it. Everything we have designed, built, and use today was possible only because we found a host of raw materials already on the planet, whether we use wood for making paper, fine furniture, and buildings; sand for making glass, cement, and silicon chips; or gold for making expensive jewelry, dental fillings, and coins. Never have we humans created something from absolutely nothing, and we never will. Clearly there is an intelligence at work in the universe that was around long before we arrived and set things up so we could play the often-silly and amateurish game called Life.

22 Carl Jung wrote *Modern Man in Search of a Soul* (1955), in which he postulates that human beings move through various stages of development. He listed and described in detail five specific levels of maturity as people get older, indicating that as you become more aware and informed, you move to a higher level of consciousness. The age groupings shown here necessarily vary greatly among individuals. The following description is based loosely on Jung's ideas.

First

Age 1–10: Adolescence: You are at the stage of the child, the age of innocence. You are dependent, impressionable, vulnerable, and compliant, meaning you are pretty much under the control of other people and the circumstances in which you find yourself. You are quite helpless and easily victimized. During this period, you are very much in the process of being molded to conform to societal wishes, beliefs, and norms (i.e., various values and virtues, as well as vices).

Second

Age 11–25: You are at the stage of the athlete. You take great pride and get a lot of your meaning from your physical appearance—your attractiveness, your beauty, your strength, your physical prowess. You sculpt your body in a gym, you tan your body in a studio, you cleanse your body in a spa, you coif your hair in a salon. Your sense of self is very much centered around this part of you and you try to stretch out this period of your life as long as possible. At various times as you age, you may take vitamin supplements, protein drinks, and steroid pills; or, more aggressively, you may undergo plastic surgery, face-lifts, tummy-tucks, hair transplants, and breast implants. But your body slowly deteriorates no matter what you do and eventually disappears into simple dust. Because this part of you is always changing, it's not real.

Third

Age 26–50: You are at the stage of the warrior. You take great pride in competing, in winning, in accomplishing, in succeeding—you strive to arrive—in proving to yourself and others that you are smart, capable, superior, and special compared to everyone else. You strive to accumulate material objects (both in quantity and quality), fill important positions in your career, and achieve goals you have set for yourself; all this then defines for you who you are. Of note is the fact that you may even go to great extremes to achieve these things. You may lie, cheat, steal, even go to the point of becoming over-stressed through overwork and put your very life at risk. This stage can be characterized by aggressiveness, manipulation, plotting, and scheming, and is often accompanied by a whole lot of ranting and raving in general. Warriors do whatever they need to do to win.

Up to this point, you are motivated mainly by fear in your life: fear of not being secure, not being accepted, not being loved, not being respected, not being able to prove you are capable and deserving, not being acknowledged as special by others for being better/faster/smarter than those with whom you compete. You then undergo a slow evolution, sometimes very slow, into being more love-motivated in your thinking and behavior. You move from your concern being primarily for me (meaning only yourself, as can be the case with many young children) to we (small and large groups including family and extended family) to primarily others (meaning everyone but yourself). In the extreme, your focus is directed totally at others, including those you don't even know and likely will never meet. This includes others who have yet to be born.

At the extreme end of the scale in one direction is a person's fixation with "getting everything and giving nothing"; at the extreme end in the other direction, it is about "getting nothing and giving everything." Then again, some people like Saint Francis of Assisi (1182–1226) and Mother Teresa of Calcutta (1910–1997) held a firm belief that is even more radical than either of these two extremes: that you get everything by giving everything away!

Fourth

Age 50-plus: You are at the stage of the statesman/humanitarian. You see well beyond the little self and feel attracted to and an intimacy for all living things. Your primary concern is for the greater good—the collective whole. Increasingly, you volunteer your services, participate in community activities, and actively support charities of various kinds.

Fifth

Age 60-plus: You are at the stage of the spiritualist and consider yourself part of the collective consciousness of humankind. You have moved beyond simple duality (i.e., the self and the Whole) to complete identification with the Divine. You are fully awake, you are fully aware, and you are fully alive. You are at one with the "universe" (aka "one song").

23 Consider love and its various meanings. *Love* as a noun is defined as: (1.) a strong affection for or attachment or devotion to a person or persons, (2.) in theology, love is God's benevolent concern for mankind and man's devout attachment to God, (3.) the feeling of benevolence and brotherhood that people should have for each other.

Love in its many forms does induce emotions of various kinds and degree. When looking at unconditional, transcendent love, however, we see that it is more than just another emotion. This state of love has a unique, mystical quality that goes beyond any emotion; in fact, it is the single, most creative force for good in the Universe.

The seat of the soul is love and what love in turn creates. To love is an active, intensely personal experience that taps into the soul's natural essence. Only transcendent love is real and only transcendent love endures. It is the ultimate expression of our true Nature.

Does love have an opposite? No. The spiritual plane does not have opposites. The absence of love is simply non-love. Everything in the physical plane indeed does have opposites: left/right, backward/forward, on/off, war/peace, before/after, open/closed, wet/dry, light/heavy, right/wrong, and so on. Thinking this way, many people believe that fear, anger, or hate is the opposite of love. It is in the physical plane. But in the spiritual plane, fear, anger, and hate do not exist. Only the ego-driven mind knows these hurtful, limiting, and debilitating emotions.

It's the same with light. Most of us think that the opposite of light is darkness. But there is no such thing as darkness per se; darkness is simply the absence of light. Hence darkness does not exist. We manifest non-love in many ways: fear, anger, hurt, hate, greed, guilt, bitterness, jealousy, resentment, and spite, all the usual litany of human failings. Ultimately, love is what each of us is seeking; it's all we want for it is all there is.

It serves no useful purpose to "know about" transcendent love simply on an intellectual level. It has to be experienced. For example, you can be taught everything there is to know about baseball—its history, its rules, the current standings, and everything in the record book. You can watch it forever yet still never really *know* it. You have to experience baseball (actually play it to win but sometimes lose) to really know what it is. It's the same with love. You have to *be* love ("pure" consciousness) and sometimes *not be* love ("self" consciousness) to fully understand and appreciate it.

24 The path to greater awareness and a higher level of consciousness can be a long and difficult one, but it is achievable. It is possible for the average individual to manifest qualities that reflect his divine Nature. Sogyal Rinpoche, in his book *The Tibetan Book of Living and Dying* (1992), explains the process of enlightenment and getting on the true path this way:

"In the modern world, there are few examples of human beings who embody the qualities that come from realizing the (true) nature of mind. So it is hard for us even to imagine enlightenment or the perception of an enlightened being, and even harder to begin to think that we ourselves could become enlightened.... Even if we were to think of the possibility of enlightenment, one look at what composes our ordinary mind—anger, greed, jealousy, spite, cruelty, lust, fear, anxiety, and turmoil—would undermine forever any hope of achieving it.... Enlightenment...is real; and each of us, whoever we are, can in the right circumstances and with the right training realize the (true) nature of mind and so know in us what is deathless and eternally pure. This is the promise of all the mystical traditions of the world, and it has been fulfilled and is being fulfilled in countless thousands of human lives."

Note: The word "true" has been added twice in parentheses for clarity.

25 The world's major religions have traditionally played a central role in society by providing spiritual guidance leading to hope, healing, harmony, and personal enlightenment. Their ultimate goal is basically the same: to help people reconnect with their essence, reclaim their inheritance, and help remake the world. Their sacred teachings show remarkable similarities in both tone and insight, as the following quotations clearly demonstrate:

* ❊ "God is the sun beaming light everywhere."
  —Tribal African; African religions

* ❊ "The radiance of the Buddha shines ceaselessly."
  —Dhammapada; Buddhism

* ❊ "God is light, and in Him is no darkness at all."
  —1 John 1:5; Christianity

* ❊ "In the lotus of the heart dwells Brahman, the Light of Lights."
  —Mundaka Upanishad; Hinduism

❋ "Allah is the light of the heavens and earth."
   —Koran; Islam

❋ "The Lord is my light; whom shall I fear?"
   —Psalms 27:1; Judaism

❋ "The light of Wakan-Tanka is upon my people."
   —Song of Kablaya; Native American religions

❋ "The Light of Divine Amaterasu shines forever."
   —Kurozumi Munetada; Shinto

❋ "God, being Truth, is the one Light of all."
   —Adi Granth; Sikhism

❋ "Following the Light, the sage takes care of all."
   —Lao-tzu; Taoism

Although there are aspects of different religions that often divide us, they also offer a universal spirituality that can unite us. Ignorance of this very fact has led to much needless violence and many atrocities throughout history.

26 Every living species on the planet cognizes its "own universe" in its own unique way. A snake uses infrared, a bat uses ultrasound, and a honey bee uses ultra-red to determine its so-called "reality." And each is able to survive as a result. In turn, humans use their own perceptual artifacts (eyes to see, ears to hear, nose to smell, tongue to taste, and skin to feel/ touch) to determine their reality, basically the nature of the physical world. And, we, too are able to survive as a result.

And your ego—that thinks because you are human, you are superior to other living things—tells you that your sensors are more accurate and hence your version of reality is more reliable, more "correct," more "real." But you know from personal experience that your sensors are often inferior to those of many animals and birds at seeing, hearing, and smelling. In fact, it has been said that human beings are able to perceive less than 1 percent of 1 percent of all that is actually there!

So here is the situation. One species sees this world; a second sees that world; a third sees another world—a fourth, a fifth, and so on, each seeing its world and each believing that what it sees is reality. But there is only one true reality, and *none of us* is actually "seeing" it. Alas, we all have imperfect sensors.

We now see that what is real cannot be perceived by physical means, regardless of the species involved. The sun never really sets or rises; the Earth is neither flat nor solid nor round; and you can never actually sit still because you live on a planet that is rotating on its own axis, circling around the sun, and also flying off into outer space at several thousand miles an hour. Yet your physical sensors would lead you to believe none of these things.

If you looked into an electron microscope, initially you would see that matter is made up of molecules, atoms, electrons, protons, and many other small atomic and subatomic particles. As you looked closer and closer to find the smallest, the most minute building block of nature, you would find that there are no more particles. There is just empty space. In fact, *all matter is made up mostly of empty space.* You therefore come to understand that the basic building block of matter is "non-matter." This non-matter is simply referred to as the void. Someone looking at you and who was able to see the "real" (physical) you, would first see something as expansive as the night sky, with emptiness everywhere, with only the odd star flickering here and there representing highly dispersed atoms. The same applies to any physical object, no matter how compact or dense you may think it is, such as the mineral called lead.

Everything in the universe is made up of the same matter; it is all made of the same basic *stuff.* There is only so much oxygen, so much hydrogen, so much nitrogen, so much carbon, so much manganese, so much silicone. Everything in nature is made up of the same basic building blocks of nature including your brain, bones, blood, cartilage, skin, and hair. As some astute observer once said, "This is that, that is that, you are that, I am that, and that's all there is!" All this stuff is simply being recycled between you and every thing and every one else in the universe. Indeed, some scientists have concluded that every living person on the planet today has one million atoms in him at any given time that were once in the body of the Buddha, Jesus, and Mohammed.

Consider these facts. As you breathe and eliminate waste, you recycle your atoms. You have a new liver every six weeks, a new stomach lining every five days, all new skin once a month, a new skeleton every three months, and on and on it goes. In fact, in less than one year you replace 98 percent of all the atoms in your body. And you replace 100 percent in two years. So to think that you are a body and only a body requires you to ask, "Which one? Which model? Is it the 1990 model, the 2000 model, the 2010 model, or this year's latest edition?" So you see that various parts of your body have a different shelf life, some quite short, some quite long. But whatever the time frame, all of it is changing all of the time.

Now it gets even more interesting. There is a part of you that has no shelf life at all; it is timeless, changeless, immortal. Each model—each new edition of "you"—carries forward memories from past experiences. Each new model remembers how to laugh or cry, love or hate, feel joy or sadness, as well as tie your shoelaces, brush your teeth, take a shower, ride a bicycle, peel an orange, toss a salad, barbecue a steak, and drive to and from work. But since you first learned all of these things, every single cell in your body has been replaced, in most cases many, many times.

It seems there is an invisible intelligence, some type of "knowing" that is in you beyond your basic physicality, beyond your simple form, beyond the world of the changing. And this intelligence is in everyone on the planet, not just a chosen few. This invisible intelligence is often referred to as your essence, your spirit, your divinity, or your soul. You can choose from any of these terms or select another one that you feel more comfortable with (after all, it isn't what you call it: It is what it is.).

Now consider this: How many other types of "knowings" might be in you that you don't remember because you have temporarily forgotten about them? I suggest that the most important memory you want to reconnect with is who and what you are, for this and only this will lead you to discover why you are here.

Clearly the spiritual and physical are not separate from one another but are very much part of each other. One represents the invisible memory or intelligence (formless) that is the "real" you; the other represents the visible carrier or host (form)—your body—of the memory itself. You have chosen to show up in the form you now have because you found it convenient for your present purposes, whatever they may be. And once your present purposes have been met, you will necessarily move on and return from whence you came.

In other words, you have come from "no-where" to "now-here" to do what you need to do; and soon you will return back to "no-where" once again, wherever that may be. Note that the letters for both of these "places" are exactly the same, just as the very essence that represents who you are is exactly the same, no matter where you are.

27 Consider human nature as we know it and witness it in action every day. The following 10 character traits (it would be easy to come up with many others) are indicative of the way we have evolved over many thousands of years. In fact, it's probably true that if we were not this way historically, we would not have survived and gone on to perpetuate others just like ourselves. Imagine a species that may have existed a million years ago that was totally selfless, and motivated only by kindness and love of humankind. How long do you think it would have survived in that environment: 200 years, 20 years, two years, two months, two weeks, two days, two hours, two minutes?

We see that these character traits represent our more primitive, primordial side—that side of our nature whose main purpose was to ensure our physical survival in earlier times. At the same time, we need to understand that some of these same character traits serve a useful purpose and can be the basis for good today.

Here are the 10 characteristics:

We are all **ambitious.** We want to advance—be more, do more, have more and better, whether wealth, fame, or respect.

We are all **opportunistic.** We tend to take advantage of situations to further our own self-interest.

We are all **stubborn.** We are obstinate; we refuse to listen or comply, preferring to stick with the status quo.

We are all **ignorant.** We don't know all there is to know about any one thing in particular or about most things in general, and never will. Hence, each of us lives our life in a huge void of uncertainty. We don't know who we are, why we're here, where we came from, or where we're going. It's no wonder, then, that we live according to something we are not.

We are all **greedy.** We have an excessive, even compulsive, desire to have or acquire; we want more than we need or deserve.

We are all **lazy.** We have a tendency to put in the least effort to get the most results.

We are all **fearful.** We have a preoccupation, a concern, a feeling of anxiety, apprehension, or agitation, sometimes even terror, relating to danger, evil, or pain, whether imaginary or real.

We are all **selfish.** We put our own interests first, well ahead of others, to an extent that is neither fair nor right nor moral.

We are all **vain.** We have and project an excessively high regard for ourselves: our ideas, our opinions, our abilities, our appearance, our possessions, and so on.

We are all **vengeful.** We want to return an injury for an injury by inflicting punishment and pain on others for what they have done to us.

If you are offended by this list, as some might be, just ask yourself: "Have I ever exhibited this particular quality at least once in my life? Have I ever been ambitious, opportunistic, stubborn, ignorant, greedy, lazy, fearful, selfish, vain, or vengeful at least once?" I already know your answer. Now we both know that each of these qualities is in you (indeed, in varying degrees in everyone), whether you want to admit it or not.

So how could some of these characteristics serve us and be the basis for good? How could they add to the collective wellness and benefit humankind? Well, you could be ambitious, opportunistic, and stubborn, and use these same characteristics to help others live healthier, longer, and more productive lives. Think of all the medical researchers who have spent years—sometimes their entire careers—to come up with cures for debilitating diseases such as diabetes, tuberculosis, and leprosy. Or inventors—where would our society be today without modern telecommunications and transportation equipment and systems? Whether modern agricultural practices, new medical devices, or new materials, all were developed to serve a very real need (although in some cases, simple greed may have been a motivating factor as well). And characteristics such as ambition, opportunism, and stubbornness will continue to drive people to use their ingenuity, creativity, and innate intelligence to better the human condition.

When other, totally selfish motives are at play, however, you need to ask the question "Why?" Why have you exhibited many or all of these traits at one time or another in your life, albeit some more frequently and more passionately than others? Specifically, what is your personal pain-story—your justification or rationalization for acting this way?

Again, may I introduce to you—the ego! The ego's power and influence over the way you think has been at work since the beginning of human history. Simply stated, it *owns* you, or at least it thinks it does. And most of us would have to readily agree because we haven't seriously considered the possibility of something else as the driving force in our life.

For example, you think, feel, and do each day without really understanding the force or forces that are directing all of this; in many cases, you do whatever you do instinctively and just hope for the best. The ego represents an elaborate belief system that is in your genetic makeup, your DNA, that first and foremost has said to you and is still saying today, "Survive! Look out for number one! Nothing is more important than your personal safety, comfort, and welfare!" And survive both you and I did. But how much longer our species will survive in the way it is currently going about it is perhaps the more pressing question.

28 To know you must survive implies you must be at risk. If you think you are at risk, you come to believe you must compete. (Sure, it's a struggle, but what choice do you have?) In order to compete, you must be prepared to fight or flee. If you fight, you might lose; if you flee, you might be caught. Fear, then, is one of the main driving forces behind a lot of what you think, feel, and do.

After telling you (1.) to survive, the ego then directs you to move up the ladder to the next level and instructs you to (2.) seek safety, security, and freedom from fear; (3.) seek acceptance, friendship, and love by associating and fraternizing with others; (4.) seek recognition, status, and self-respect; and finally (5.) to prove to yourself and others that you are unique, capable, and worthy of high achievement. Having gotten you this far, the ego tells you with great fanfare that you have finally "made" it; you are now on top of the world! And it takes full credit for getting you there! This scenario loosely describes Abraham Maslow's hierarchy of human wants and needs as first postulated in his book *Motivation and Personality* (1954).

The ego in you is always focused on building up the ego for the ego's sake (i.e., selfish concern for me) and is totally incapable of considering more altruistic pursuits (i.e., unselfish compassion for others). Its primary goals are twofold: self-aggrandizement and survival. This must be kept top of mind when considering how the ego works. In other words, it is enemy number one (in the sense that it wants to control and direct all your thoughts, feelings, and actions) and must be recognized as such.

Maslow's ideas are usually depicted as part of a large pyramid with five distinct levels: *Physiological* needs are at the very bottom, rising to *safety* needs, *social* needs, *self-esteem* needs, and ending with *self-actualization* needs at the top. Maslow's theory in this regard is central to helping us understand our basic desires and motives for wanting more in our life. In this regard, the key question we must always ask is: "What is my real motivation for wanting more?" Is it simple self-interest (selfishness) or society's general welfare (selflessness)? Or can the former also lead to the latter? Hmmm. What do you think as it applies to what you are trying to accomplish in your life?

Later in life, Maslow postulated that his pyramid shouldn't stop at self-actualization needs at the very top, that in fact there is another key factor he had unwittingly left out. This he called *transcendence,* meaning the spiritual level that transcends the purely physical world. Maslow's transcendence level recognizes our natural desire to act morally and ethically with compassion, humility, empathy, kindness, tolerance, benevolence, and generosity. Without taking into account this spiritual or trans-egoic side to our nature, he felt we are simply living as instinct-driven animals or pre-programmed machines.

An important factor that initially gave credibility and power to the ego, and continues to do so today, is that you were born as a single entity. You discovered that you came in a certain "package" or container, so to speak: a body with finite walls that were made of soft, delicate skin. You arrived in this body very much separate from every thing and every one else. Quite quickly—in fact instantly—you also found yourself all alone. This, at a time when you were the youngest, weakest and most vulnerable, is a very scary realization indeed!

But it gets even worse. Your actual physicality—your physical form—allows you to use only physical sensors to perceive what you see as only a physical world. Now, as you look out and observe all that is going on around you, your separateness is confirmed: Yes, you are separate; yes, you are alone; yes, you are at risk; yes, you must compete; yes, you must fight; and yes, there is good reason to be afraid. (Yes, those train tracks do come together somewhere off in the distance!) We are all wired—7 billion–plus people—to think this way; we are all driven instinctively to want more and more out of life, and eventually get to the so-called "top." Knowing this, should it be any surprise that there are so many problems in the world?

The ego evolved as a necessary survival mechanism for individual human beings during the long and arduous course of human history. And it did its job very well, at least for those of us who are here today. The irony is that now it has become more of a death wish. As such, we must find ways to overcome or transcend it, not just tame it or try to control it, as it now clearly threatens both our individual and collective selves.

As we humans develop more and more efficient and innovative ways of killing each other (i.e., IEDs, cluster bombs, and unmanned, missile-carrying aerial drones), and more and more invasive ways of degrading, indeed raping, the planet (i.e., open-pit mining, clear-cutting forests, and bottom-trawling the ocean floor), there is an urgency today that has never been greater in history. Whether we are able to change our ways, to rise above our destructive nature, only time will tell. Many think it is already too late.

29 We have previously described the 10 character traits that are a product of the ego, or are at least closely connected to it. In contrast, consider other traits that are beyond the ego, in fact unknown to the ego, examples of what we will call *supreme virtue*. They are prime examples of our true Nature. It may be that we don't see them on display in the world as often as we would like but when we do, we usually take special notice of them. (Here the late Nelson Mandela comes to mind.) These traits or qualities go by such names as honor, respect, compassion, empathy, humility, honesty, truthfulness, virtue, courage, industriousness, justice, righteousness, fairness, generosity, service, responsibility, forgiveness, mercy, and unconditional love.

This list is by no means complete but it's a good beginning. Let's see what each of them means:

Honor: A keen sense of right and wrong; adherence to actions and principles that are considered right.

Respect: To feel or show honor or esteem for others; consider or treat others with deference or courtesy.

Compassion: To feel sorrow or deep sympathy for the troubles or suffering of others, with an urge to help.

Empathy: The projection of one's own personality into the personality of another in order to understand him better; intellectual identification of oneself with another.

Humility: The state or quality of being humble of mind or spirit; absence of pride or self-assertion.

Honesty: Refraining from lying, cheating, or stealing; being truthful, trustworthy, and upright.

Truthfulness: Sincerity, genuineness, honesty; the quality of being in accordance with experience, facts, or reality.

Virtue: General moral excellence; right action, and thinking; goodness of character.

Courage: The ability to face anything recognized as dangerous, difficult, or painful; quality of being fearless or brave.

Industriousness: The putting forth of earnest, steady effort; hardworking; diligent.

We now see how you can live authentically, meaning in a genuine and real way as opposed to a false and hypocritical way. *You need only manifest the divine essence that is within you.* To live authentically is to live in agreement with fact or actuality, in a manner that is consistent with who and what you are. When you are authentic, and only when you are authentic, can you be useful to a higher cause; in other words, play this game called life with much more insight, much more skill, and much more passion. This involves love: love of self, love of others, and love for all things, both animate and inanimate.

The only alternative is to stay trapped into trying to prove to the world that you are a "somebody," indeed a special somebody. The irony is that you don't even know who this somebody is that you are pretending to be. It's like every day is Halloween and you don a different costume that you think best suits the occasion: "Hey, do you like me like this? No? Then how about this? Or this? Or this? Please, like *some* version or variation of me!"

Hypocrite means: (1.) an actor, one who plays a part; (2.) a pretender; an imposter; (3.) a person who pretends to be what he is not; (4.) one who pretends to be better than he really is or pious, virtuous, etc., without really being so.

When you live thinking you are a human being having an occasional spiritual experience, (for example, adopting virtuous behavior only when it suits you and the circumstances), you have to ask yourself, "Am I really what I portend to be?" In other words, is being spiritual only a part-time job? At a deep, subconscious level, you know you are not; you are living falsely, dishonestly, and inconsistently. In fact, you are living a lie.

Yes, a lie that you have been led to believe by authority figures, caretakers, and well-wishers of all kinds who constantly told you to do this but do not do that; believe this but do not believe that; act like this but do not act like that; go to this church but do not go to that church; enjoy doing this but do not enjoy doing that, etc. And you have never seriously questioned all of their dictates. These people, after all, were much older and wiser than you, and supposedly had your best interests in mind; shouldn't they know?

All professional actors live a lie when they perform on a stage and take on the persona of someone they are not. And it is an extremely difficult and stressful undertaking, to which most would readily attest. Now consider spending all of your waking moments pretending you are someone you know you are not. This results in a serious case of cognitive dissonance: You are aware there is a disconnect. You say to yourself, "I don't like this game; I'm not very good at playing this game; I don't want to continue playing this game." You show your displeasure by resorting to the usual primitive behaviors that result from disappointment, frustration, and anger; you lash out, you criticize, and you complain. Yes, you demonstrate all the usual mean-mindedness, even invectiveness, that is indicative of the fact that you are not happy.

Everyday *happiness* is defined as having, showing, or causing a feeling of great pleasure, contentment, joy, or gratification. And for many, to be happy is the primary purpose of life. But real, authentic happiness is not fleeting, nor is it something that can be had indirectly. Rather it is the result of a deep *knowing* that comes from being and doing what is in accordance with who and what you are. It's when you are in a state of continuous validation of your very essence, living as your true Self.

In other words, authentic happiness is not a by-product of something else. You cannot buy it, steal it, eat it, drink it, or touch it as an entity in its own right as many thieves, con artists, fast food addicts, alcoholics, drug addicts, and sex addicts would have you believe. It can be had only directly, with no strings attached. Happiness is an energy and a force, and not a result of anything physical in the world. You can never hope to put your hands around it, caress it, and say, "Wow! Look: I finally have this thing called happiness."

Here is a keen observation by popular American singer and comedienne Margaret Young (1891–1969): "Often people attempt to live their lives backwards: they try to have more things or more money, in order to do more of what they want, so they will be happier. The way it actually works is the exact reverse: You first must be who you really are, then do what you need to do, in order to have what you want."

30 Consider these words by Lama Surya Das in his book *Awakening the Buddha Within* (1997) about how to move beyond your first impulse, the ego:

> "As you walk the inner path of awakening, recognize that it is most definitely a heroic journey. You must be prepared to make sacrifices, and yes, you must be prepared to change. Just as a caterpillar must shed its familiar cocoon in order to become a butterfly and fly, you must be willing to change and shed the hard armor of self-centered egotism. As compelling as the inner journey is, it can be difficult because it brings you face-to-face with reality. It brings you face-to-face with who you really are."

31 So how should you go about living your life? There are two principal ways you can gain some insight into what you could do and how you should behave. One way is to watch others whom you admire, and then try to emulate, copy, or duplicate their behavior. This option is called *modeling,* because you are using a model (an actual picture or image) as a prototype for your own actions. And it works quite well. Athletes use it, actors use it, and singers and dancers use it.

Of course, this approach has some limitations. First, you may not be witnessing what the other person is doing in a perfect way. Second, you may not have the natural talent and ability the other person has, and hence cannot do exactly what the other person has done. Third, a perfect model for what you want to do may not exist, or at least may not be readily available to you. And fourth, you may not possess the same motivation, self-discipline, and intensity as the model does.

The second way involves creating a picture in your mind of the precise behavior you want to exhibit. This approach is called *creative imaging,* because you are relying on your imagination and intellect to define the specific behavior you want to adopt. This approach also has its limitations.

First, some people are not very good at forming mental pictures—they may be more verbal and less visual in the way they think. Second, mental pictures are less specific in nature; at best, they are an approximation of the behavior you want to emulate. And third, as in modeling, you simply may lack the natural talent and ability, as well as the motivation, self-discipline, and intensity you need in order to do what you are visualizing in your mind.

Most people make use of both these approaches in their daily life. Consider the evolution of a child. A child's mother (or father) may be a teacher, a nurse, or a singer. A child's father (or mother) may be a policeman, a fireman, or an actor. We all know children who grew up and adopted the same career paths as one of their parents; they ended up doing what they witnessed on a daily basis.

We also know children who became as adults what their imagination created for them. Walt Disney was interested in cartoons when this art form was still in its infancy. The Wright brothers were interested in airplanes when none had yet been built that actually flew. Thomas Edison was interested in electric light at a time when only candles were available. Alexander Graham Bell wanted to use copper wire to transmit the human voice over long distances when such an idea was considered totally absurd. Yet through trial and error and total faith in themselves and in what they wanted to do, they all succeeded.

Clearly, whether you rely on various role models that are available to you or the creativity and ingenuity of your own mind, you can achieve a very high level of competency if you really believe in the thing you want to do. This applies to all areas of human endeavor: art, literature, engineering, sports, business, politics, entertainment, as well as practicing spirituality and integrating its powerful principles into your daily life.

In this regard, some questions come to mind. Is there a spiritual teacher with whom you are familiar, admire, and would like to emulate? Is there a unique contribution you would like to make to others—and ultimately to your self, since we are all One? Where does your real, intense, waiting-to-be-manifested passion lie? The only way to answer these and other questions like them is to go into silence and listen attentively to what it tells you. As the Buddha counseled us many years ago, "Your work is to discover your work, and then with all your heart to give yourself to it."

32 Consider beliefs (in particular, yours!), how you got them, and how they currently influence the way you think, feel, and act (in precisely this order) on a daily basis. Like everyone else, you have a very detailed and extensive belief system that is deeply embedded in your mind, and you use it to observe, understand, and define yourself and your place in the world. In most cases, you have become totally comfortable with it, and therefore no longer question it or even know that it exists.

For example, you have probably come to like certain people and not like others; to like certain foods and not like others; to like certain cars and not like others; to like certain books, movies, clothes, jewelry, and jokes, and not like others. It could also be said that not only have you become comfortable with these personal frames of reference, you have become a slave to them. They are forcing you to limit yourself to thinking inside a box of a certain size. Again, if you feel compelled to challenge or dispute this statement, this is proof by itself that you are limited in how you think.

Let's look at the belief system you now have that defines for you much of your basic make-up: who you are; what you're made of; why you're here; what you stand for; what strengths, talents, and natural abilities you have; how to behave; what dreams and aspirations you should have; and so on. In other words, you have adopted a certain mind-set, a certain sense of self, a certain self-identity, a certain self-concept, a certain notion of who you are: how attractive, how capable, how acceptable, how lovable, how intelligent, how productive, and therefore how important and how worthy you are. This is how you have allowed your brain to be programmed up to now. And guess what? This book is going to ask you to question this master paradigm and change it—indeed, change it dramatically in some important areas.

To ask you to change your personal belief system—how you see yourself, your world, and your place in it—is often viewed as an exceedingly challenging, even daunting task by many people. Remember before we proceed that we have all had to make paradigm shifts—both major and minor—in our life concerning our beliefs about any number of things, both big and small. For example:

* ❋ On October 14, 1947, Chuck Yeager became the first person to break the sound barrier in an airplane. Many thought this could never happen.

* ❋ On May 6, 1954, Roger Bannister became the first person to run the four-minute mile. Many thought this could never happen.

* ❋ On July 20, 1969, Neil Armstrong was the first person to walk on the moon. Many thought this could never happen.

* ❋ In the early 1990s, Japan entered an economic recession after almost 40 years of rapid economic growth. This recession went on for more than a decade, and well into the new millennium. Many thought this could never happen.

* ❋ On September 11, 2001, terrorists flew two commercial aircraft into the Twin Towers of the World Trade Center in New York City, destroying both structures and taking approximately 3,000 lives. Many thought this could never happen.

* ❋ On October 10, 2002, a single share in Nortel Networks (a much-respected high-tech firm) closed the day on the New York Stock Exchange at 67 cents. It was valued at more than $124.00 (or 12,400 cents!) only 24 months earlier. Many thought this could never happen.

❋   During the last quarter of 2008 and first quarter of 2009, some economists estimate that between $10 to $15 trillion evaporated into thin air as a result of the global banking and credit crisis. Many thought this could never happen.

Add to this list the fact that when you look down a set of train tracks, they appear to come together somewhere off in the distance. But when you get on a train and travel that distance, you find that they do not. In other words, what you see on the physical level is not actually real!

So perhaps the task at hand—changing your concept of who and what you are—is not as daunting as you first thought. Consider this comment by the American writer Elbert Hubbard (1849–1912): "The recipe for perpetual ignorance is to be satisfied with your opinions and content with your knowledge."

33 Here is a quote from the book *Jonathan Livingston Seagull* (1970) by Richard Bach:

"The only difference, the very only one,

between those who are free and the others,

is that those who are free have begun to understand

what they really are and have begun to practice it."

This is one of my favorite books, and it contains only 127 pages. I recommend it to you. It is about an extremely brave and daring young seagull named Jonathan Livingston Seagull who *thinks* he is an eagle.

Here is my take on the story. We know all seagulls who think they are seagulls do what other seagulls do; and we know all eagles who think they are eagles do what other eagles do. So Jonathan, believing he is an eagle, acts accordingly. He hovers at great heights, he soars above mountaintops, and he dives at frightening speeds, all the dramatic and often dangerous things that eagles do. Not surprisingly, his fellow seagulls think he is completely mad and kick him out of the flock. But is he really mad?

Think about it. Because he thinks he is an eagle—it is what he conceives and believes himself to be—and for this reason only, Jonathan is able to do pretty much all the things that eagles do. What a great metaphor for you in your life!

You now know what you have to do: Decide who you want to be and what you want to do. Do you want to hover at great heights and soar above mountaintops? Do you want to be the best you can be? Do you want to do something significant, and contribute something unique and meaningful to help others in the world who are hurting?

You can if you *think* you can! It only requires that you formulate the appropriate pictures in your head, then act on them with immense passion, unbridled self-confidence, unlimited determination, sharp focus, and an unwavering commitment to succeed.

34 Here is what three world-renowned experts have said about critical aspects of your psychological make-up: your personal belief system; your self-image; and your level of self-esteem. These factors are all closely related and interdependent, and each plays an important role in your life.

"What is self-esteem? It is how a person feels about himself. It is his overall judgment of himself—how much he likes his person. A person's judgment of self influences the kinds of friends he chooses, how he gets along with others, the kind of person he marries, and how productive he will be. It affects his creativity, integrity, stability, and even whether he will be a leader or follower. His feelings of self-worth form the core of his personality and determine the use he makes of his aptitudes and abilities. His attitude toward himself has a direct bearing on how he lives all parts of his life. In fact, self-esteem is the mainspring that slates each of us for success or failure as a human being."

—Dorothy Corkille Briggs,
author of *Your Child's Self-Esteem* (1970)

"There are positive correlations between healthy self-esteem and a variety of other traits that bear directly on our capacity for achievement and for happiness. Healthy self-esteem correlates with rationality, realism, intuitiveness, creativity, independence, flexibility, ability to manage change, willingness to admit mistakes, benevolence, and cooperative-ness. Poor self-esteem correlates with irrationality, blindness to reality, rigidity, fear of the new and unfamiliar, inappropriate conformity or inappropriate rebelliousness, defensiveness, over-compliant or over-controlling behavior, and fear of or hostility toward others.

"The higher our self-esteem, the more ambitious we tend to be, not necessarily in a career or financial sense, but in terms of what we hope to experience in life—emotionally, intellectually, creatively, and spiritually. The lower the self-esteem, the less we aspire to and the less we are likely to achieve. Either path tends to be self-reinforcing and self-perpetuating."

—Dr. Nathanial Branden,
author of *The Six Pillars of Self-Esteem* (1994)

"The 'self-image' is the key to human personality and human performance. Change the self-image and you change the personality and the behavior. But more than this. The 'self-image' sets the limits of individual accomplishment. It defines what you can and cannot be. Expand the self-image and you expand the 'area of the possible.' The development of an adequate, realistic self-image will seem to imbue the individual with new capabilities, new talents, and literally turns failure into success."

—Maxwell Maltz, MD,
author of *Psycho-Cybernetics* (1960)

Dr. Maltz explains that psycho-cybernetics is a mental activity that takes place at all times and in all circumstances as you live your life, whether you want it to, know it, accept it, or not. This is important to understand, as you spend almost all your waking moments thinking about any number of things, from what to eat for breakfast in the morning to what time to go to bed at night.

This is how your mind actually works to get you through each day. The conscious mind is a goal-seeking mechanism—it's called teleological or psycho-cybernetic—and it represents a unique success system that never fails. It takes a picture stored in memory and transforms it into its physical counterpart, just like a modern camera creates an actual photograph from a visual image. The mind has been designed and built to do this perfectly and consistently; in fact, it is incapable of not doing this. This is the principle regarding all purposeful human behavior: Your mind *always* acts out the pictures you have put in your head.

The implications of this phenomenon are both prophetic and profound. If you want to be successful at any given activity—parenting, managing, selling, public speaking, or losing weight—you have to have the right pictures stored in memory regarding that particular activity. It's a simple equation that basically says only positive inputs produce positive outcomes.

These positive inputs—pictures!—represent a detailed imprint or blueprint for being successful at whatever it is you are trying to do. The process begins with a diligent and thorough search to find the right pictures—this could be called the *applied* part—then accepting them as valid and true for you, as representing who you really are; this could be called the *surrendering* part.

It's important to ask yourself what pictures come to mind as you consider the questions "Who am I?"; "What am I made of?"; and "Why am I here?" These pictures are critical as they are an indisputable and significant indicator of where all your thinking has taken you in your life. They are also the major driver buried deep in your subconscious that is determining the direction your life is now taking. Once this assessment has been done, you will be in a much better position to make positive changes.

So where can you find the *right* pictures and what can you do to readily access them? As we have seen, they come from no-mind—from the depths and tranquility of Now. This is why you are encouraged to engage in meditative practice every day. In stillness, as your mind begins to shed its many preconceived (often-silly) ideas, (often-silly) understandings, and (often-silly) concerns, these pictures begin to appear as you are in your most basic, natural, and simplistic state (i.e., unconditioned consciousness). You realize this is who you are, that this is your very essence. When you understand who you are, then fully accept and closely identify with who you are, you begin to act out this reality in all that you think, feel, say, and do. *At last!* The shackles of your prior conditioning have been broken. You are free and able to embrace a new reality.

35 If you were God and had all the powers available to you that God has—to radiate, to illuminate, to communicate, to educate—what would you do with your life? What pleasures would you gladly forsake? What initiatives would you eagerly undertake? What contributions would you earnestly make? Ah, yes, if only you were God. (Okay, if you want to notch it down a bit: if only you were *God-like!*)

36 Clearly there is a point where a person sees beyond his individual nature and private needs and wants. Here, such a person is "at one" with spirit, hence is totally "need-less" and "self-less" in his thinking and behavior. This level can be called "Unity Consciousness." Buddhists would say that if you were at this level, you could ignore all the others, that in fact there is only one level of true consciousness. They would say that the other levels are only temporary diversions/distractions along the true path to Oneness or nirvana.

Nirvana in Buddhism is the state of perfect blessedness achieved by the extinction of individual existence and by the absorption of the soul into the supreme spirit; it involves the elimination of all earthly desires and passions.

The late Maharishi Mahesh Yogi (1918–2008), the founder of Transcendental Meditation, was once asked the following question at a public event: *"Maharishi, wise people everywhere know that 'As you sow, so shall you reap.' And mystics are fond of saying that we are all one. If there is literal truth to these sayings, then whatever you do to another person you must be doing to yourself. Therefore, as you have said, violence has no value* to solve problems. *My question is, how literally can we take these sayings that we are all one? We seem to be separate, but is there some higher reality that we are not perceiving? Are we like individual cells in one body?"*

The Maharishi answered: *"Exactly like that. I think your inference is grand. All are one. The example will be of a tree—so many thousand leaves, thousand branches, thousand flowers, fruits and all. They are all different on one level—they are one on another level. They are one on the level of the sap—they are different on the level of the expressions of the sap."*

37 I believe it is possible to tell how successful you will be in your life by asking the following five questions, and then critically assessing your answers. They are in no particular order except I would put the last one first!

1. What are your dreams/goals?
2. Who do you associate with?
3. How do you spend your spare time?
4. What books are you reading?
5. What values do you live by?

38 We have seen that cognitive-behavioral therapy (CBT)—itself a form of critical thinking—has been used for more than 50 years by leading psychiatrists and psychotherapists all over the world to treat people suffering from either mild, moderate, or severe depression. Unfortunately, depression is one of the most prevalent yet most difficult diseases in our society to treat. Many people (including teachers, doctors, nurses, lawyers, bankers, soldiers, police officers, politicians, actors, singers, musicians, etc.) don't even want to admit they are feeling depressed because of the social stigma (i.e., embarrassment and shame) that is associated with it. Most decide to just tough it out and keep on keeping on, hoping that things will get better all by themselves. Because the disease is often never admitted to, it's seldom properly treated, leaving people to endure their pain all alone and in the silence of their own mind.

The *Toronto Star* reported some interesting results in the first countrywide survey on mental health in Canada (with a population of about 31.5 million at the time) in an article on September 4, 2003. It found that 2.6 million people (1.4 million women and 1.2 million men) reported having symptoms of mental illness (i.e., about one in 12 people). Symptoms were related to anxiety, bipolar disorder, schizophrenia, major depression, eating disorders, and suicide attempts. Of this number, almost half, or 4.5 percent, reported symptoms or feelings associated with major depression. Mental illness was found to be 18 percent for people aged 15 to 24, 12 percent for those aged 25 to 44, 8 percent for those aged 45 to 64, and 3 percent for seniors 65 and older. Fewer than half sought out any treatment.

Here's another important finding. The results of a 16-week study at the University of Pennsylvania on the effectiveness of cognitive therapy were published in the April 2005 issue of the U.S. journal *Archives of General Psychiatry*. The study involved 240 people with moderate to severe depression. One group of 60 received cognitive therapy; another group of 120 received antidepressant medication (usually Paxil); and a third group of 60 received a placebo or sugar pill. The finding was that cognitive therapy when provided by experienced psychotherapists was just as effective as antidepressant drugs in the initial treatment of moderate to severe depression.

According to the researchers, patients in the cognitive therapy group attended two 50-minute sessions each week for the first four weeks of the study, one to two sessions a week for the next eight weeks, and one session a week for the final four weeks. After eight weeks of treatment, the response rate was 50 percent in the medication group; 43 percent in the cognitive therapy group, and 25 percent in the placebo group. After 16 weeks, the response rate was 58 percent for patients in both the medication and cognitive therapy groups.

The researchers concluded by saying, "It appears that cognitive therapy can be as effective as medications." This finding was contrary to the guideline at the time of the American Psychiatric Association that said most moderately and severely depressed patients required medication.

39 Another study shows how science is only now catching up to spirituality. Scientists have discovered that a single cell found in a microscopic piece of skin, flesh, or cartilage has the DNA of the whole species contained within it, whether a human being, a plant, or an animal. In recent years, we have seen the first cloned sheep; Dolly was born on July 5, 1996. She was followed by a mouse, a pig, a cat, a rabbit, a cow, and a horse. Then, on April 23, 2009, scientists announced they have cloned a puppy that even glows in the dark! They named him Ruppy, short for Ruby Puppy (Source: Wikipedia).

In other words, the son or daughter created exactly as the father or mother. Think about it. A fertilized cell of a living organism can replicate all the parts of the original organism; the intelligence of the whole is contained in the smallest particle of the whole. Does this not say something profound when you consider the wisdom of universal mind (i.e., the intelligence of the whole) being contained in you (i.e., the smallest particle of the whole)?

40 There is an incredible Presence or *knowing* that lies deep inside each of us. We often hear its pleadings—its gentle whisper calling us home, wanting to reunite us with the joy, peace, and love that it represents. But we seldom heed its call. Perhaps it's because we are afraid of it; after all, it is unknown to most of us. Or perhaps we think we can heal ourselves—that we are strong enough or smart enough to overcome anything that ails us.

We all have issues from the past, which can make us feel trapped or limited. These can be manifested in our daily life in many ways, including hurt, fear, anger, guilt, or regret. Certain preoccupations may also be at play. We may lack confidence in our ability to live our life the way we think we should; indeed, we may want to live a life completely different from the one we are now living. We may wonder why there isn't more love, hope, meaning, and sense of purpose in our life. We may be suffering from the recent loss of a loved one, a debilitating addiction, a marriage breakup, or the loss of a job that we have had for many years. Or perhaps it is the fear of our own death that frightens us the most; we know we are all going to die sometime (i.e., undergo yet another transformation!).

As this is happening, many of us find we cannot heal ourselves all by ourselves. We know another power, whose magnitude we can only guess at, is also at play, yet we often live in ignorance or denial of this very fact. Perhaps we feel unworthy, weak, or inept because we are unable to do this. We may even feel ashamed of our seeming incompetence. After all, we do solve a large number of problems of various kinds every day. So the ego, never too far from our innermost thoughts, tells us to just labor on, learn a little more, try a little harder, become a little smarter—but no matter what, never surrender!—all representing false hope, wasted effort, and poor logic. The result is, and can only be, ongoing pain and suffering. What a dilemma—yet what an opportunity to grow if we would but wake up!

41 Here is a quote from *A Course in Miracles* that talks about what is real and what is true: *"Truth is unalterable, eternal, and unambiguous. It can be recognized, but it cannot be changed. It applies to everything that God created, and only what He created is real. It is beyond learning because it is beyond time and process. It has no opposite, no beginning, and no end. It merely is."*

42 Can practical spirituality help you with goal-setting in your life? After all, we are always settings goals of one kind or another, but very often we don't achieve them.

The answer is a definite *yes!* The first and most important consideration when goal-setting is to ask yourself, "What is my motivation, my real purpose, for wanting this result (i.e., whatever goal you have decided upon) in my life?" You can answer this question by imagining you have already achieved this goal—that it's already part of your life. This way, as an internalized entity and existing in Now, you will be able to sense how it feels in your gut, and in turn come to understand if the goal is primarily for personal and selfish reasons or for the common good. It's a significant difference in how you feel. If it's indeed appropriate for you, it will resonate with your energy field and excite you like nothing else can. This, invariably, is why such goals are ultimately achieved: All this positive energy is directed at them and not at others.

When living in the world of form, we tend to organize everything in our life as perfectly as we can, like lining up all the ducks at a shooting gallery. To this end, we set goals, goals, and more goals, both major and minor. We then spend an inordinate amount of time each day trying to achieve them: Get this (object/thing) in place, get this (object/thing) in place, get this (object/thing) in place.

As a young woman, for example, you may decide to marry your boyfriend, move to California, and pursue an acting career. On the few occasions when we are successful at getting everything absolutely perfect—note this only adds to the illusion that we can organize our external affairs exactly the way we want all the time and all by ourselves—we sit back and marvel at how great our life is. "Wow," we say, "I've finally made it. What a smart person I am!"

But in the world of form, we know the phenomenal nature of events and situations is totally unpredictable and sometimes tragic. So one day everything can indeed be fine and the next day everything can be terrible. It's like asking for more cards (by tap, tap, tapping on the table) in a poker game, trying to come up with a perfect hand (i.e., a royal flush). We want to get everything just right; we want to win the jackpot. But when even one of these cards is missing (the ace, for example), things necessarily fall back into total disarray. What a way to live!

Imagine you are Captain Edward John Smith and have just been selected as the first captain of the RMS *Titanic,* the culmination of a long and illustrious career as a naval officer. You are asked to take this fine ship, the largest and most sophisticated ocean liner in the world at the time, on its maiden voyage. The ship is slated to leave Southampton, England, on April 10, 1912, on its way to New York City. Incredible—what an honor!

The result? On top of the world one moment, at the bottom of the ocean the next! (Captain Smith chose to go down with his ship.) Win an Academy Award one moment, enter drug rehabilitation the next. Win the MVP at the Super Bowl one year, be relegated to warm the bench the next. Win the lottery when you are 25, be penniless and homeless at 30. Get married in Las Vegas on Saturday, get divorced in Tahoe on Sunday. Such is the nature of living in the extreme, polarized environment of "object" consciousness.

43

Let's revisit spirituality and try to understand why interest in it is on the increase in many parts of the world at the same time that interest in organized religion, at least in many parts of the West, is in decline. Spirituality can be defined in many ways. I see it as acceptance that there's an element of the sacred in each of us—that there is a world beyond the world of form, beyond what we can perceive with our five senses. It's recognition that we are more than just our physical bodies and the thoughts we think. It's through spirituality that many people find meaning, hope, comfort, and peace of mind. Ultimately, spirituality is about understanding our relationship with the Infinite, and taking steps to develop and nurture that relationship.

There are many paths to enlightenment, and each and every religion is potentially one of them. At the same time, many people are finding that organized religion, at least in the way it is being practiced today, isn't meeting all of their needs and aspirations. This group is seeking a more direct, meaningful, and experiential relationship with the Divine.

And that's their choice. Spirituality, of course, doesn't require you to give up your religion or any religious beliefs you may have. It's not a matter of either this (my religion) or that (the spiritual path). It's just another step—albeit for some an extremely important one—to consider as you travel down the road to greater awareness and a higher level of consciousness. (As has been shown in the text, many of the world's major religions have common spiritual themes and practices that they all share, honor, and celebrate.)

Here is something people are beginning to understand if you remain locked into or obsessed with the everyday world of form: You are limited—there is absolutely no doubt in this regard—to bouncing back and forth between pain and pleasure, disappointment and elation, over and over again. Up one day, down the next; this is the most you can ever hope for. The result? The experience of pure joy and everyday bliss will always escape you. Therefore some people decide to move on, going deeper and deeper in search of something that is more helpful, meaningful, and impactful—indeed more enriching and fulfilling for them.

There are several benefits that people find as a result of spiritual awakening. So let's see how spirituality is able to bring such benefits into our life. People who are spiritually aware clearly understand two remarkable things. First, they know they cannot find in the world of form—no matter how long or how frantically they search—what exists only in the formless (namely peace, love, hope, joy, and bliss), and second, they know they cannot find in the past or future what exists only in Now (namely understanding, meaning, acceptance, contentment, and fulfillment).

❋————————————————

> People who actively practice spirituality are able to evolve naturally and with minimum effort. They are more at ease with themselves and their world. They are more content, creative, productive, perceptive, and empathetic, and are more in harmony with others and with nature. They find it easier to make decisions, adjust and change, set priorities, and manage their affairs. They feel more inter-connected and grounded, and less controlled by old habits and past conditioning. They manifest pure joy and experience great bliss, which is their true Nature. Personally, I see it as a get-out-of-jail card; you are literally being set free!

————————————————❋

Spiritually aware people are able to live in such a way that their life situation never takes them over completely, regardless of the extremes of the pain-pleasure spectrum. Because such people are centered at their core, their pain is never so crippling or debilitating (i.e., "My world is a total disaster!") that they want to do themselves or others any harm, and their pleasure is never so euphoric or overwhelming (i.e., "My world is absolutely perfect!") that they feel they are on top of the world. It's because whichever way it is today, they know that tomorrow it could well be very different or even the exact opposite!

It has been said that some people live by the light, meaning with an inner glow. Imagine this as a candle that is in you. When you are spiritually connected, the flame on this candle is burning and shines brightly. It never brightens, it never dims, and it never goes out completely. It just shines brightly.

Now, as each day arrives, you lift the curtain of your mind to this new dawning, this new day. Some days, you find that the sun outside is shining brightly; other days, you find that a storm is in full force. Each represents one end of the two extremes that always applies in the world of form (e.g., up/down, over/under, hot/cold, stop/go, etc.). Neither of these occurrences has any impact on you, however, as your inner candle continues to shine brightly. So you simply proceed to go about your day. Whether the sun is shining outside or not (i.e., whether your life situation is favorable or unfavorable, welcomed or not welcomed), you function as you should, knowing what you know, being who you are, and doing what you need to do.

A final analogy to emphasize this point: When you look at any large body of water such as the ocean, you see that the surface is always in a certain state of disarray and disruption; invariably, there are waves of some kind. These may be small ripples, sizable undulations, or large white-caps, depending on the wind and other weather conditions at the time. On the other hand, you know that whatever is happening on the surface, if you travel down to the bottom of the ocean, to the very depths of the ocean, everything there is calm, everything is peaceful, and everything is serene.

And so it is with your everyday life. On the surface, meaning the world of form, everything there is active, busy, in flux, and in motion. But while all this is going on, if you travel down to the depths of your mind, into silence, into stillness, into the world of no-form, you will find there that everything is also calm, everything is peaceful, and everything is serene.

This is why people flock to the oceans and lakes of the world in the first place. There, it is much easier to kick back, relax, and be your Self. In such a place, close to water, close to nature, there is much less competition in the way of inner ego and outer stimulation to keep your mind constantly running in overdrive.

44 The *Wall Street Journal* on November 7, 2013, commented on the dramatic increase in loneliness in the United States. It is thought that high divorce rates, more single-family households, electronic (remote) rather than in-person communications, the retirement of the Baby Boom generation, and more elderly people in our ranks with a variety of health issues all contribute to the problem.

The article cited John T. Cacioppo, a psychologist and director of the Center for Cognitive and Social Neuroscience at the University of Chicago, who analyzed several large studies on loneliness. He estimates the level of loneliness has doubled in the past 30 years, with about 40 percent of Americans report being lonely today, compared to only 20 percent in the 1980s.

The article also noted researchers at Brigham Young University who studied the correlation between social relationships and mortality in 2010. In a meta-analysis of 148 studies involving more than 300,000 participants, here is what was discovered: "[L]oneliness was as strong a predictor of early death as was alcoholism or smoking 15 cigarettes a day, and it was a stronger predictor than obesity or a sedentary lifestyle." (See the section subtitled "Love" on page 152 for effective ways to deal with this challenging and unfortunate social trend.)

45 We all need to better understand *romantic love* because of the important role it plays in our personal life—indeed in our modern society. After all, the family unit traditionally has been the cornerstone of our social order. What is romantic love, anyway? Why do so many people crave it and feel that life is a total waste without it? Why does it bring so much happiness to some, and so much pain and sorrow to others? With divorce rates in many countries hovering around 50 percent, it appears that something is tragically amiss.

Perhaps a little background is in order. In today's world, we see an enormous fixation on the material aspects of life—again, the world of form—from fancy cars, to designer clothes, to over-sized homes, and the belief that these things can make us happy. This is problem #1. We can call it the "toys-and-trinkets" factor.

There is also the aspect of instant gratification, especially by the younger generation, the wanting of things that are seen as desirable right now, immediately, if not sooner! This is problem #2, the stress, anxiety, and depression, or S-A-D, factor. This mind-set places enormous pressure on people and often leads to conflict between couples, usually as a result of too much debt.

Then there is the status factor, our compulsive and often-repulsive need to prove to the world (and ourselves) over and over again how important, how smart, how capable, and how attractive/lovable we are. This is problem #3, the "prima donna" factor.

With these things just described all happening at the same time, our lives are necessarily in overdrive, with everyone wanting to get somewhere (in fact nowhere) as quickly as possible. We know a treadmill leads you nowhere, after all. It only causes you to break out in a sweat while standing still!

And the liberation of sexual mores and practices in many countries continues unabated. As a result, we see higher and higher instances of teenage pregnancy, sexually transmitted diseases, single mothers, single households, and common-law marriages, as well as an ever-increasing divorce rate in North America and elsewhere. To note, the United States has the highest divorce rate in the Western world (Source: Wikipedia).

As Bob Dylan told us back in 1964, "The times they are a-changin'." And we know they are changing faster today than ever before. To deal with these developments, however, we as responsible and caring adults need to better understand the many social and psychological forces that are at play.

I offer the following observations regarding romantic love. They are not meant as a criticism or judgment in any way. In other words, I'm not saying romantic love is either good or bad, or somewhere in between; I'm only saying that it needs to be better understood.

We know romantic love is a euphoric experience of monumental proportions, indeed a magnificent blessing, a unique and enthralling experience quite unlike any other we can hope to have in our lifetime. Unfortunately, however, though we readily welcome such feelings, they often blind us concerning what is really going on. So let me try to explain "what is really going on."

We all experience different kinds of love in our life, and they include transcendent love, familial or family-centered love, and romantic love. Regarding the latter, romantic love, we have seen in the text how the ego is always wanting and needing—always trying to complete and better itself. This is the dynamic, then, that is taking place when two people find each other physically and emotionally attractive, and "fall" in love.

The attractive part is the primitive, primordial sex drive we all have that perpetuates our species. The often-called chemistry that causes us to find one person more attractive than another is the luck of the draw, I believe. It's something we are born with and must contend with as best we can.

People who are in love feel that when they are together, they are better off, meaning more happy, playful, and joyful—more alive! But we must come back to what is real, to what is permanent, to what never changes. And by this criteria, romantic love by itself is neither real nor permanent, although it may be more convenient for a time for many personal and societal reasons (like having a ready sexual partner and the raising of children).

But we know many people fall in and out of love; it comes, it goes, it intensifies, it diminishes. Others may remain in love all their lives. It doesn't matter. With the death of both parties, it comes to an end (i.e., when a person dies, the ego in that person dies, along with anything and everything that the ego helped create). I suggest, then, it could be argued that every marriage that is based solely on romantic love is simply a marriage of convenience.

As an aside, we know there are other marriages that are devoid of any kind of love at all. This makes them also marriages of convenience. Here the reasons may be to reduce living expenses or have simple friendship or companionship. It's not unlike having a roommate in college.

Romantic love usually involves two very different people coming together with very different ego-related and trans-egoic drives. We know these drives often change with age and maturity; one person may change in one or more of these areas while the other may change in other areas or indeed in none at all. It comes down to how well such aspects of the two people allow them to co-exist as a unit for the mutual benefit of both. In this sense, marriage is very much an ongoing exercise in adjusting, in accommodating, in compromising, with the hope that staying married keeps you in a better place.

A final comment: Can you imagine being a gentleman who is head over heels in love with a lady you absolutely adore, but she decides to marry someone else? (I certainly can; it happened to me.) If you truly loved this person, wouldn't you be the first to step up and cheer her on, knowing she believed she would be happier in this other relationship? (Are you kidding? I can't imagine doing that!)

Of course, you also might think she was wrong in making the decision she made. (Yes, I sure did!) And you could very well be right. (It turned out that I was.) But is this not the ego in you jumping in, making its presence known, and putting your self-interest first and foremost? (Okay, okay—I plead guilty on all counts!)

In a typical "romantic love" marriage, the convenience factors could include any or all of the following: (1.) safety and security; (2.) acceptance and friendship; and (3.) recognition, status, and self-respect. In fact, there is no end to what the ego wants for you and no end to its telling you that it can provide it. The constant and persistent message it impresses upon you is "Do exactly as I say and you'll get everything you want!" Until you find a ready response to this most alluring—but highly misguided—entreaty or learn how to ignore it, I believe you are putting yourself and your well-being at serious risk.

I offer the following as the ideal situation. As we have just seen, every purely "romantic love" relationship has a large ego-related component embedded deep in it that is a key part of its dynamic. And we know that dueling egos don't make for pleasant conversation, good company, or easy living, let alone a happy marriage. So what elixir or other ingredient could be added to calm the waters that would bring kindness, patience, empathy, and understanding to the situation? Consider this: What if you were to bring unconditional, transcendent love—where the ego plays absolutely no part—into the relationship as well? Then you would have something quite remarkable—indeed, something very, very unique. In this instance, you would have nothing less than pure, enthralling, ever-enchanting bliss! And bliss has magical powers attached to it as it allows miracles to show up—yes, *miracles*!—not just once or twice, but on a regular basis.

Miracles are very interesting things, even though you may not have experienced many of them in your life up to now. (You very likely have but weren't able to see them for what they are!) So what are miracles, anyway? Miracles are remarkable, unforeseen occurrences that seemingly defy natural law and hence are thought to result from some supernatural power. And, strange as it may seem, miracles have very little—in fact, nothing—to do with you individually and everything to do with the world at large (i.e., the One Consciousness). In other words, they are not "personal" in the sense that they occur for only one person's benefit; they are a collective happening, a collective event, and have an omnipresence and omni-effect.

> "All that is required now is that you continue to till the soil of your soul. Just as you would not neglect seeds that you planted with the hope that they will bear vegetables and fruits and flowers, so you must attend to and nourish the garden of your becoming."
>
> —Dr. Jean Houston,
> American philosopher and social scientist;
> author of *A Mythic Life: Learning to Live Our Greater Story* (1996)

What if You Stopped Playing a Role? (Annex 13)
The best conversation often involves the fewest words.

You are addicted to assuming a multitude of roles as you go about each day. For example, you may assume the role of a shopper or salesperson, a giver or taker, a teacher or student, a sister or brother, a mother or daughter, a father or son, an employer or employee, and so on. You have all these roles perfected or down pat, as we say. They have become part of your ingrained behavior, your so-called "natural" way of Being. Yet these roles you play are far from being natural. Instead, they are contrived and artificial, like an elaborate game. They are more a defense mechanism you use to protect yourself than an authentic and true expression of who and what you are.

What a dilemma! By acting in such robotic, preprogrammed ways, you are hiding your true Nature from both yourself and those with whom you regularly interact. It's like you are an actor who enters the stage of life each day and repeats a number of roles assigned to you by your manipulative, egoic mind. You simply adopt a particular role you think best suits a given situation. But what would happen if you deleted all this old, worn-out programming and began anew—if you embarked on an exciting yet perhaps quite scary path of rediscovering who you are?

Consider the following. Can you imagine being totally present while in the company of an old acquaintance, a close friend, a loved one, or even a complete stranger? This means you need only "be" (i.e., allow what is and completely surrender to that), which precludes playing a role of any kind, whether that of a friend, a mentor, a lover, or business associate. It's clearly a whole new way of engaging with a fellow traveler.

In this regard, consider adopting a sort of passive-attentive stance in the way you communicate with the other person. Instead of the usual type of interaction (talking, laughing, gesturing, clapping, and adopting a wide variety of facial expressions and body positions), you communicate mainly by way of the *feelings* (love, compassion, understanding, and gratitude) you are experiencing deep inside on a daily basis (i.e., 95 percent of the time).

The more you do that, the better you do that and the more naturally you do that, the more you will learn about who and what you are. In addition, you are more likely to discover these same things about the other person. When all the masks are thrown away, when all the pretenses are dropped, when all the usual platitudes are discarded (a process of getting naked), it's very revealing and empowering to see what shows up.

Highlights of this Book (Annex 14)

Everyone has experienced a moment in simple stillness, one without thinking "I am this" or "I am that." Here, only the realization of "I am" rang true and real.

Consider the following list. Here you will find some things you already know—and perhaps didn't even know you knew—and for these you need only a gentle reminder to make you aware of them again. Regarding some other things, you just have to figure them out for yourself. I hope I have assisted you on both counts. The goal is always to live a positive, peaceful, and purposeful life, one that is full of meaning and fulfillment.

You must:

1. Know who you are.
2. Know you are totally responsible for every aspect of your life.
3. Know you create your own reality.
4. Know the power of your basic beliefs and adopted values.
5. Know you have no limits as well as unlimited opportunities.
6. Know you must discover your passion—your own area of excellence.
7. Know how to define what success means for you.
8. Know you are love, only love, and need to fully internalize and externalize that love.
9. Know how to see beauty, God's gentle fingerprint, in every one and every thing.
10. Know you must serve.

Definition of Success

Success is measured by the proportion of your full potential that you dedicate and direct to the betterment of other people and the planet.

"If you correct your mind, the rest of your life with fall into place."

"Every human being's essential nature is perfect and flawless, but after years in immersion in the world, we easily forget our roots and take on a counterfeit nature."

"Of all that is good, sublimity is supreme. Succeeding is the coming together of all that is beautiful. Furtherance is the agreement of all that is just. Perseverance is the foundation of all actions."

"The snow goose need not bathe to make itself white. Neither need you do anything but be yourself."

"To the mind that is still, the whole universe surrenders."

—Lao-tzu (c. 604–531 BCE),
founder of Taoism;
author of *Tao Te Ching*

The Mind T.R.A.P.

"A human being is born as an absolute egoist, and this quality is so visceral that it can convince him that he has already become righteous and has rid himself of all egoism."

—The Talmud (Hagiga)

The student asks:

"Master, can you explain what the 'joy of awakening' is one more time?"

The Master replies:

"No, I cannot. I suggest you go into the place of no-mind and simply be, and find out for yourself."

The student asks:

"Master, how can I find my true Self?"
(i.e., enlightenment)

The Master replies:

"Lose your little self."
(i.e., stop identifying with your mind and assuming you are it and it is you)

How to Avoid the Mind T.R.A.P.

Ultimately, to be unhappy, judgmental, intolerant, or angry is to deny the existence of God and your own divine Nature.

It is important to know how to identify and deal with the possible illogical, irrational, inaccurate, or improbable nature of any particular thought you may have. The goal is to avoid the Mind T.R.A.P. This is where you often consider a thought to be 100 percent true when in fact it may well be totally false. The exercise described here represents a relatively quick yet effective method that uses critical thinking to weed out thoughts that need to be eliminated from your mind, and thus stopping them from impacting your consciousness and negatively affecting your mood and subsequent behavior.

In every case, you will find that the inquiry in question simply takes the ego out of the situation and replaces it with humility, understanding, acceptance, and love. For if you see things happening to you or around you that you don't particularly like, want, or agree with, then in a very real sense you are pretending to be the Almighty and acting as though only you know the truth, meaning what is right or wrong about a given situation. Of course, when the ego is at the center of the equation, none of us can know the truth, or what is right or wrong about any situation. And to think we can only leads to unnecessary and unwanted pain and suffering. Invariably, arrogance, ignorance, presumption, and false pride (all aspects of the ego) lie at the center of all false beliefs.

The Mind T.R.A.P. works something like this. Assume you witness an event or are part of a situation that upsets you or makes you angry at either yourself or the world. You then formulate a statement of some kind in your mind that portends to accurately describe what you have just witnessed or experienced. However, you do a very bad job of it because you do this while in a weakened and unstable (i.e., ego-infested) cognitive state. The result represents an unfortunate double-whammy: You end up both upset/angry *and* stuck with a faulty statement/narrative that you believe justifies your hurt. To correct this predicament, there is only one recourse available to you: You have to calmly and deliberately *deconstruct* what you have just built. In other words, you have to come up with an exit strategy that brings greater logic, accuracy, and rationality back into the equation. Only then can you move ahead with clarity, wisdom, and understanding, with empowering and uplifting attributes that represent your higher Self.

The inquiry involves the following four questions you need to ask to check the relevancy and accuracy of any given thought, notion, idea, or understanding you may have about a situation you are faced with:

T.	Is the thought 100 percent *t*rue?	Yes	No
R.	Is the thought 100 percent *r*elevant?	Yes	No
A.	Is the thought 100 percent *a*ccurate?	Yes	No
P.	Is the thought 100 percent *p*roven?	Yes	No

Assume you have a thought that is causing you some dismay, distress, anxiety, pain, regret, or even anger of a certain magnitude. Take a piece of paper and carefully write it down. For example:

My thought says:

Is the thought 100 percent true?

Is the thought 100 percent relevant?

Is the thought 100 percent accurate?

Is the thought 100 percent proven?

Now, with this statement in mind, systematically ask the four pertinent questions, carefully consider your answers, and then write them all down.

Obviously, if you determine that the thought is *not* 100 percent true, *not* 100 percent relevant, *not* 100 percent accurate, or *not* 100 percent proven, this means that there is no reason to hold on to it. To do so is only keeping you in an unwanted, unproductive, and unhealthy state. So you need to throw the thought away faster than you can say, "Get out of here!"

What does this exercise actually accomplish? Specifically, it helps you identify when you might be using prejudgments, total absolutes, over-generalizations, oversimplifications, gross distortions, simplistic ratio-nalizations, or false assumptions, all known enemies of critical thinking, to formulate a certain statement in your mind that describes from your perspective the situation as you see it. "Probabilities" are a critical fac-tor here. For if there is any chance, even an extremely small one, that the statement you have in mind is not true, not relevant, not accurate, or not provable, then you have overstated your premise and mistakenly assumed it to be fact. Thankfully, by seriously questioning its accuracy and valid-ity, you have determined that it is fiction and hence no longer needs your continued attention.

Once the thought has been found to be false, for example, something quite remarkable takes place and it is *immediate*. Instead of the hurtful, stressful, or sometimes-angry feelings you had before when you assumed your thought was 100 percent true, a whole new set of feelings arises and impacts your consciousness. They include compassion, understanding, peace, joy, serenity, and love. These then becomes your new reality.

Examples to Illustrate the Point

In Presence, there is only peace. In ego, there is only pain. So...where would you rather be?

1. A distraught daughter might be saying:

"My parents don't listen to me; they don't understand me; they don't care about me. This can only mean they don't love me."

Note: Inquiry here may prevent a depression or an attempted suicide.

2. A disgruntled employee might be saying:

"My boss doesn't like me; he doesn't respect me; he doesn't appreciate the good work that I do. He probably thinks I shouldn't even be working here."

Note: Inquiry here may prevent a verbal outburst or an act of physical violence.

3. An angry father (perhaps born somewhere in Asia) might be saying:

"My daughter (perhaps born somewhere in North America) is no good; she is ignoring her culture and heritage; she dances, she smokes, she has a boyfriend, and she dresses like all her other friends. She is an embarrassment to me and our whole family."

Note: Inquiry here may prevent an ugly confrontation, a physical beating, or even an honor killing in a fit of rage.

Explanation

Consider the narrative in the first example just presented (a distraught daughter) and let's conduct the suggested analysis together. This way, we can determine whether the final conclusion that the daughter has reached is indeed true or false, correct or incorrect, fact or fiction.

* "My parents don't listen to me." Beginning with the first question in the Mind T.R.A.P. exercise, "Is the thought 100 percent true?" we can see that it may be true on some occasions but certainly not on *every* occasion. Undoubtedly, there have been times when her parents did listen to her. Therefore, we can stop here and move on. This is because if any of the four questions is shown to be incorrect (i.e., not true, not relevant, not accurate, or not proven), it totally negates the final conclusion.

* "They don't understand me." Again, when we ask the first question, we get the same result; namely it may be true on some occasions but certainly not on *every* occasion. So we can stop here and move on.

❋ "They don't care about me." Again, when we ask the first question, we get the same result; namely it may be true on some occasions but certainly not on *every* occasion. Again, we can stop here and move on.

❋ At this point, our focus shifts to the final conclusion that was reached by the daughter: "This can only mean they don't love me." In this particular example, we have determined all the statements that supposedly support this conclusion are not true. This makes the conclusion itself also not true.

Hence, the daughter has to realize that her thinking represented in this example is faulty and illogical, and her final conclusion is not supported by the facts. Upon knowing this, she is free; any and all suffering she was experiencing is necessarily negated and instantly disappears. Clearly her ego played a large part in the formulation of her narrative and this, in turn, precipitated the anger and hurt that followed.

Many people have narratives like these still haunting them in their life today, and are continuing to suffer needlessly and endlessly as a result. Therefore they need to systematically conduct the Mind T.R.A.P. exercise on each and every one of them, whether the incident in question goes back several years, perhaps even to their childhood, or indeed applies to a situation that exists today.

M aster Your Mind, Master Your World

The quality of your consciousness each moment determines the quality of your life each day. This tells us a great deal just how precious Presence actually is.

The Top Five Insights of Very Enlightened People (Annex 15)

The average life has two parts. The first half is mostly spent in the fast lane, frantically feeding the ego. The second half is mostly spent in the slow lane, trying to find your soul.

At this point, having read the text, you have been exposed to well over more than hundred sacred truths and insights that are common to all very enlightened people. Naturally, certain ones will resonate with you more than some others, so you can choose the ones that seem more consistent with your own basic beliefs, experience, and personality. In other words, you may wish to compile your own "top five" list and use these as your personal markers or sign-posts as you go about living your life. Alternatively, you may consider adopting the ones described here.

1. They have come to understand, accept, and practice who they are, what they're made of, and why they're here. In other words, they live authentically, consistently, and in harmony with their true Nature.

2. They live in the present, in each moment, in Now. Here, in this place, they see that all things are in fact perfect exactly as they are—that nothing, anywhere, is wrong or incorrect. They see only perfection all around them, in every aspect of their life and their world.

3. They accept that everything (some good/some bad) happens for a reason and a purpose, and in each and every case, it serves them. It may not serve them today, tomorrow, or even five or 10 years from now, but eventually, in the long run, they know it will serve them.

4. They accept that their Source is all loving, all powerful, and all knowing. By understanding their Source, identifying with their Source and becoming one with their Source, they, too, take on these same attributes.

5. They see only love in all things and in all situations. In other words, they live above the fray, above the inconsistent, unpredictable, and incongruous nature of the physical world. They understand only love matters, that it is the essence of their Being and the energy that sustains them.

The top five insights listed here create a meaningful and practical path to follow, indeed a way to live a life full of peace, hope, happiness, serenity, and inner joy. Very enlightened people are able to follow this path because they have the ability—and *know* they have the ability—to manage the way they think (i.e., using both "active" and "passive" thinking) on a minute-to-minute and day-to-day basis. This way, they control their feelings and actions.

As a result, they have created a reality that is more consistent with what is true and what is real. As such, they are able to be authentic to who and what they are, regardless of what is happening to them or around them. They are able to say to themselves and others, with deep and unwavering conviction, "All is well in my mind, all is well in my heart, and all is well in my world." Their journey home is complete. Their search for everyday bliss is over.

Better People, Better Community

The student asks:

"Master, why should we seek enlightenment?"

The Master replies:

"A parent, a teacher, a doctor, a judge, a soldier, a police officer, a swim coach, a scientist, a politician, a business manager, an architect, a nurse, a salesperson...would they not all be better at their profession if they were also better as a person?"

There is nothing wrong with who you are; this is pure perfection. The error is who you think you are; this is pure conjecture, pure fantasy, pure nonsense.

You think you can manage the known and the unknown. In fact, you cannot. For you will always experience pain when there is some distance between Truth and who you think you are, between Self and your notion of your self.

It takes an enormous amount of energy to be a "somebody." You have to maintain the charade, live up to expectations, keep on script, and stay consistent with every aspect of your story. It takes no energy at all to be your Self.

Powerful Pointers to Truth

"The Self alone exists; and the Self alone is real.
Self is only Being—not being this or that. It is Simple Being.
BE, and there is the end of ignorance....
If one can only realize at heart what one's true nature is,
one then will find that it is infinite wisdom, truth, and bliss
without beginning and without end."

—Sri Ramana Maharshi (1879–1950),
Indian Spiritual Master

C
O
N
C
L
U
S
I
O
N

Pointers to What Is True and What Is Real

"Whatever satisfies the soul is truth."

—Walt Whitman (1819–1892),
American poet, essayist, and journalist;
author of *Leaves of Grass* (1855)

1

*Love is simply recognizing
the sacred in another, in fact
the same sacred
that is in you in another.*

2

*When you live authentically,
in alignment with your Source,
you will naturally mirror the love that is your Source.
You will see the futility of being anything
other than who you really are.*

3

*Whenever you feel pain yourself, any pain,
or inflict pain on others,
you have forgotten who you are.
You are asleep and need to wake up.*

4

*Your Source knows only good;
by being an instrument of this good,
you are contributing to the collective wellness
of all those close to you
and through them, to all of humanity.*

5

When the love in you
recognizes the love that is in another—
what is your very essence—
that's "it," that awareness is "it"!
The "it" is the sacred
and that sacred is in you!

6

Take 15 minutes and
go into silence; try to see the
many facets of Oneness
of a simple, stoic frog
sitting patiently
on a shiny, green lily pad.

7

You cannot hope to do great things
until you know
you have greatness within you.

8

Where do you think all great thoughts—
of wonder, of revelation, of hope—
come from, both big and small? From silence, of course.
Can it be any surprise, then, to discover that
this is where God also resides?

9

When you find love and become that love,
you will have found your true Self.

10

All real growth involves
the attraction and internalization of divine energy
and the manifestation of its power and relevance.
The objective is always service—
the giving of gifts for the common good.

11

All your searching, confusion, doubt, and anxieties
will disappear when you discover
who and what you are—love, unlimited love.
This knowing—
that you are love—
allows you to know you are worthy of every blessing,
every kindness, every thing.

12

Unconditional love is the one connecting link
you share with all living things.
It is literally embedded in your DNA.

13

When you recognize and embrace your very essence,
and accept it as who you are,
the more abundance of every kind will appear
in your everyday life, especially love.
For once you have found it, it has found you
and will manifest itself through you.
As a result, your life will never be the same.

14

*The mind is always looking for meaning
and direction, its identity, its very essence.
If it fails to find this in truth,
it will find it in form, in falsity, in frivolity.
In other words, it will find it in EGO.*

15

*Remember that your Self or true Nature
is not something that is false or fabricated
or phony or fluctuating. It is constant, pure, natural,
and authentic. It is incorrupt and permanent. It is real.
It is also something you dearly love and
want to know more about; in fact, you want to become
intimate with it, to become one with it.
Why? Because you know when you are real, you are home.
And when you are home, you are at peace.*

16

*The power that is represented
in "all that is" is also in you.
It includes empathy, understanding, hope,
compassion, resiliency, patience, enthusiasm,
tolerance, resourcefulness, creativity, optimism—
all the glorious manifestations of love.*

17

*A raindrop is happy indeed
when it enters a stream;
it is even happier when it becomes
part of a mighty river;
and it is as happy as it can be*

when it flows into a vast ocean.
For to become one with your Source
is to come home again,
and home is where you know you are loved
for simply being who you are.

18

Everything that happens in your life is
not meant to cause you distress and hardship
or even joy and elation;
it is meant to wake you up!

19

A powerful mantra, affirmation, or prayer
is simply to say, "Thank you."
With heartfelt conviction.
You should say it at least one hundred times a day
as you go about "being" and "doing."
This tells every one and every thing
in the Universe how much you love them.
Love is that place where you know
we are all One.

20

Just having an intellectual understanding
that you are love really doesn't change things.
The change comes when you actually know and apply
this truth to a given situation. When you are hurt,
when you are ailing, when you feel inadequate or flawed,
these are the times you need to let love in
and flow through you. To "be" you.
Love heals all wounds. It comforts your soul.
It renews you in every way.

21

Many people think, "I am not good enough,"
"I am inadequate," or "I am flawed."
And the ego is fine with all of this. Why? Because if
you buy into these beliefs, this kind of thinking,
you are doomed. You are at the mercy
of the ego and it will dictate the terms of
every aspect of your life.
The result? It is the master and you are its slave.
You have surrendered your essence
and your Being to false ideas, silly notions,
to beliefs that are simply not true.

22

Any movement, any religion, any point of view,
if it tries to explain itself using only words,
is at risk of being misunderstood.
That's because each word by itself is a potential error.
Words by their very nature are only words,
and are totally incapable of conveying
the full meaning of what is intended.
Of course, words can point, describe, infer and imply,
but they are a poor substitute for the real thing.
So what is the real thing?
It is that which is experienced directly and personally,
and deeply touches the soul.

23

Here is the lesson: Whenever you feel anything—
sad, hurt, angry, jealous, fearful,
upset, lost, rejected, ignored, or depressed—
other than deep peace, which is your natural state,
it is telling you something important.

It is telling you that you have forgotten who you are!
You just had a thought that has a large ego component
buried somewhere in it, and you are not the ego.

Your task is now clear:
Find this ego component and promptly take it out.
All of it. (It's called an egoectomy.)
Once you do this, the particular negative feeling
you were experiencing
dissipates and simply goes away.
It has been dissolved; it no longer exists.
You are free!

24

Your normal state of awareness
can best be described as unconscious or asleep
because you have no idea who you are.
You are simply being consumed and distracted
by a preoccupation with both mind and matter.
You are oblivious to Now, you are oblivious to Being,
and you are oblivious to your Source.

In this, the unconscious state,
you are not the one who is using your mind.
Far from it. It is the ego that is using your mind and
for no useful purpose other than to satisfy
its own selfish interests and demented desires.

25

You need to know that feeling hurt or depressed
on occasion has a greater purpose behind it.
It tells you that your thoughts are not in alignment with truth.

*Consider this: Feeling hurt physically sends you
a strong message: Don't touch that hot stove!
And feeling hurt emotionally also sends you
a strong message: Your thinking is irrational or illogical;
it's all wrapped up in the ego.*

*When you finally see what is going on,
you come to realize that this suffering had to happen
to wake you up. And once in this, the enlightened state,
you are able to see beyond the petty fray,
the mundane minutiae of everyday life to a new frontier,
a new understanding. Now, with this as your vantage point,
your new perspective, you are better able to see your role
in the greater scheme of things:
It is to help humankind rise up and prosper.*

Allen, James. *As a Man Thinketh* (London: Free
    Library, 1902).

Almaas, A.H. *The Unfolding Now: Realizing Your True
    Nature Through the Practice of Presence* (Boston,
    Mass.: Shambhala Publications, Inc., 2008).

Bach, Richard. *Jonathon Livingston Seagull: A Story* (New
    York: The Macmillan Publishing Company, 1970).

Beck, Aaron, A. John Rush, Brian F. Shaw, and Gary
    Emery. *Cognitive Therapy of Depression* (New York:
    The Guildford Press, 1979).

Benson, Herbert, MD. *The Relaxation Response* (New York:
    William Morrow, 1975).

Bodian, Stephan. *The Impact of Awakening: Excerpts From
    the Teachings of Adyashanti* (Los Gatos, Calif.: Open
    Gate Publishing, 2000).

Boswell, Nelson. *Inner Peace, Inner Power* (New York:
    Random House, 1985).

Burns, David D., MD. *Feeling Good: The New Mood Therapy*
    (New York: Avon Books, 1980).

Chopra, Deepak, MD. *Buddha* (New York: HarperCollins,
    2007).

A Course in Miracles (New York: Penguin Books, 1975).

The Dalai Lama. *The Art of Happiness at Work* (New York:
    Penguin Group, 2003).

Das, Surya. *Awakening the Buddha Within: Tibetan
    Wisdom for the Western World* (New York: Broadway
    Books, 1997).

BIBLIOGRAPHY

Doidge, Norman, MD. *The Brain That Changes Itself* (New York: Penguin Group, 2007).

Dyer, Wayne W. *Your Sacred Self* (New York: HarperCollins, 1995).

———. *There's a Spiritual Solution to Every Problem* (New York: HarperCollins, 2001).

Ellis, Albert, and Robert A. Harper. *A New Guide to Rational Living* (Englewood Cliffs, N.J: Prentice-Hall, 1961, 1975).

Giblin, Les. *How You Can Have Confidence and Power* (New York: Prentice-Hall, 1956).

Hahn, Thich Nhat. *Be Still and Know: Reflections From Living Buddha, Living Christ* (New York: The Berkley Publishing Group, 1996).

Hay, Louise L. *You Can Heal Your Life* (Carlsbad, Calif.: Hay House, 1999).

Kabat-Zinn, Jon. *Full Catastrophe Living: Using the Wisdom of Your Body and Mind to Face Stress, Pain, and Illness* (New York: Delacorte Press, 1990).

———. *Wherever You Go, There You Are: Mindfulness Meditation in Everyday Life* (New York: Hyperion, 1994).

———. *Coming to Our Senses: Healing Ourselves and the World Through Mindfulness* (New York: Hyperion, 2005).

Kapleau, Philip. *The Three Pillars of Zen,* revised and expanded edition (Garden City, N.Y.: Anchor Books, 1980).

Katie, Byron. *A Thousand Names for Joy: Living in Harmony With the Way Things Are* (New York: Random House, 2007).

Lao-tzu. *Tao Te Ching: A New Translation* (Boston, Mass.: Shambhala Publications, 2005).

Liebman, Joshua Loth. *Peace of Mind* (New York: Simon and Schuster, 1946).

Maharaj, Nisargadatta. *I Am That* (Acom, 1973).

Maltz, Maxwell, MD. *Psycho-Cybernetics* (New York: Prentice-Hall, Inc., 1960).

Millman, Dan. *The Four Purposes of Life* (Novato, Calif.: New World Library, 2011).

Ruis, Don Miguel, MD. *The Four Agreements* (San Rafael, Calif.: Amber-Allen Publishing, Inc., 1997).

Selby, John. *Seven Masters, One Path* (New York: HarperCollins, 2003).

Seligman, Martin E.P. *Learned Optimism* (New York: Alfred A. Knopf, 1990).

Simpkins, Alexander C., and Annellen M. Simpkins. *Principles of Meditation: Eastern Wisdom for the Western Mind* (Boston, Mass: Tuttle Publishing, 1992).

Smith, Douglas, and Kazi F. Jalal. *Sustainable Development in Asia* (Manila, Asian Development Bank, 2000).

Smith, Huston. *The World's Religions: Our Great Wisdom Traditions* (New York: HarperOne, 1958, revised 1997).

Thomas, Christina. *In Tune With the Soul* (Solana Beach, Calif.: Chela Publications, 1992).

Thoreau, Henry David. *The Illustrated Walden* (Princeton, N.J.: Princeton University Press, 1971).

Tolle, Eckhart. *The Power of Now* (Vancouver, B.C., Canada: Namaste Publishing, 1997).

———. *Stillness Speaks* (Novato, Calif.: New World Library, 2003).

Vardey, Lucinda. *God in All Worlds: An Anthology of Contemporary Spiritual Writing* (New York: Pantheon Books, 1995).

Walsch, Neale Donald. *Conversations With God: An Uncommon Dialogue,* Book One (New York: G.P. Putnam's Sons, 1995).

Watts, Alan. *The Way of Zen* (New York: Vintage Books, 1957).

Williams, Mark, John Teasdale, Zindel Segal, and Jon Kabat-Zinn. *The Mindful Way Through Depression: Freeing Yourself From Chronic Unhappiness* (New York: The Guilford Press, 2007).

Williamson, Marianne. *A Return to Love: Reflections on the Principles of a Course in Miracles* (New York: HarperCollins, 1992).

Yogananda, Paramahansa. *Inner Peace: How to Be Calmly Active and Actively Calm* (Los Angeles, Calif.: Self-Realization Press, 1999).

Walter Doyle Staples has been touching people and changing lives for more than 30 years through his insightful writing and passionate teaching. His journey into self-discovery began as a young adult when he suffered from stress, anxiety, and depression, then methodically and purposely went about finding ways to deal with that. As a result, he was able to overcome this limiting aspect of his life and went on to become an Air Force officer, a career diplomat, a corporate executive, a college professor, as well as a professional speaker and highly acclaimed author.

Walter points out that being successful doesn't always make you happy but being happy always makes you more successful. He explains that true and lasting happiness—*authentic* happiness—is a result of knowing who and what you are, and using this to pursue your valued goals and cherished aspirations. People who are already happy seem to possess unique characteristics that include optimism, and the creativity and enthusiasm it spawns; likeability, and the respect and support of others it engenders; and openness and flexibility, and the cooperation and loyalty it generates.

Walter has spent half of his working career in the United States, and half in Europe and Canada. He teaches worldwide, speaking to clients in business, government, non-profits, healthcare, law enforcement, the military, and academia. The goal is always to help men and women achieve the highest level of success in both their personal and professional lives. His previous books include *The Greatest Motivational Concept in the World* (1985); *Think Like a Winner* (1991), now available in 14 foreign languages in more than 45 countries; *Power to Win* (1994); *In Search of Your True Self* (1996); *Everyone a CEO, Everyone a Leader* (2000); *May the Healing Begin* (2010); *The Hollywood Cure for Stress, Anxiety and Depression* (2011); and *Park Bench Odyssey: How I Found Enlightenment in Simple Stillness* (2012).

The author may be reached at info@walterdoylestaples.com.